Christmas Past in Essex

Christmas Past in Essex

ELIZABETH WALLACE

First published in 2007
by Tempus Publishing

Reprinted in 2008 by
The History Press
The Mill, Brimscombe Port,
Stroud, Gloucestershire, GL5 2QG
www.thehistorypress.co.uk

British Library Cataloguing in Publication Data.
A catalogue record for this book is available from the British Library.

ISBN 978 0 7524 4463 5

Printed in Great Britain

Contents

Acknowledgements

Special thanks to Sylvia Kent who provided so much material, help and guidance. I also appreciate my husband, Donald Wallace, who never wavered in his energy, enthusiasm and technical skill, all of which I needed to complete this book.

I am very thankful to the following people who have contributed to the contents of *Christmas Past in Essex*. I apologise to any individual or organisation that I may have inadvertently forgotten to mention. Every effort has been made to obtain full copyright for all materials used in this book, but should I have been negligent in some areas, please accept my sincere apologies.

Linda Arthey, Jack Bartlett, PC Jo Bennett, Nola Bloor, George Booth, Martin Ambrose & Mary Bray, Reverend Elwin Cockett, Susan Cussen, Councillor Tony Cussen, Dickens Fellowship, Dan Eagle, Mike Edmonds, Beverly Egan, Essex Pig Farm, Essex Record Office, Theresa Francis, Mr and Mrs Christopher Friend, Ginny Gibson, Simon Gibson, Evelyn Gladstone, Robert Gladstone, Clara Hall, Sarah Henderson, George Hopkins, Linda Hyams, Dawn Hyde, International Lions and Rotary Clubs of Maldon, Peggy Iris, Queenie Jackson, Sylvia Kent, Peter Kent, Claire Knott, James Merriott, Reverend Ronald Messenger, Oldchurch Hospital, Derek

Oliver, Richard Peacock, Humphrey Phelps, Roger Pickett, Margaret Powell, James Reddell, Dennis Rookard, Salvation Army, Barbara Sanderson, Jim Shrubb, Tim Smith, Fred Smith, Anne Sparks, David Sparks, Rachael Tappenden, Ian Thurgood, Unilever, Doreen Waters, Sybil Watt, Linda Weiss, Dorothy Whisker, Wilkin & Sons, Jan Williams, Joyce Burgess, Clacton Sailing Club, Essex Tourism Office, Joan Merriott, Betty Pether, Patricia Pound, Saffron Walden Museum, Society of Women Writers & Journalists, Shirley Tollliday, Eileen Ward.

Introduction

The landscape of Essex with its ancient villages and towns, rolling hills and rugged shorelines does not appear to have changed drastically over the centuries. What has changed are the people going about their daily lives constantly adapting to the environment. The people of Essex have always been hardworking, strong-willed individuals with a clear sense of responsibility and a high work ethic. Perhaps this stems from generations past who migrated from London eastwards searching for a new place to raise their families and build a new life.

We can safely assume that when these people arrived in Essex, they brought many rich and wonderful traditions, customs and superstitions that are still practised every day. Many of these can be seen at special times of the year, notably at Christmas, Boxing Day and the New Year.

Cromwell tried in vain to stop the celebrations of Christmas Day in Essex by having the church doors locked, and thereby denying access for those who wished to worship. Instead, people took to their homes and invited their neighbours and family to rejoice and celebrate this special time. Their homes were decorated with evergreens collected from the countryside, they made special foods and drinks so it seems that even Cromwell could not extinguish the spirit of Christmas in the hearts of Essex people.

As I collected the fascinating and intriguing stories in this book, I was reminded of the injustice of the classes – the 'haves' and 'have-nots'. We can see how the minority lived in their manor houses giving extravagant parties and balls. On the other side, we see the majority who made up the working class and how they eked out a living and still did their best to provide a pleasant Christmas for their families.

Most of the stories included are warm and hopefully thought provoking, from the young girl living in an orphanage who remembers vividly how Christmas affected her life, to the young boy whose family took in prisoners of war and served them Christmas dinner.

Hopefully, readers will recall similar memories from their childhood and perhaps some will write those memories down for future generations. I was pleasantly surprised at the generosity and openness of those who shared their precious memories and photographs with me. I am mindful of the responsibility placed in my hands to make sure these memories and photographs are properly documented for their families and history.

Christmas, and the lead up to it, is such an important time in our lives that many people remember fondly an event, a new addition to the family, or a special present from mum and dad who had worked so hard to pay for that present. I hope this book will help rekindle some of those happy memories.

People, Places and Events

The Dagenham Girl Pipers

Christmas is often the busiest time of the year for the Dagenham Girl Pipers. Some members will appear at local pantomimes while others may have travelled half way across the world to appear at some other important function. Miss Peggy Iris, one of the first pipers, recalls that some of the most memorable events were when appearing in front of our own royal family, but she also remembers appearing for the King of Norway, Prince Leopold of Belgium, Adolf Hitler and Eleanor Roosevelt, First Lady of America.

The concept for the Dagenham Girl Pipers began with an intriguing idea by Reverend Graves who ministered at the Dagenham Congregational church in Osbourne Square where he also ran a Sunday school programme for his parishioners' children. The Reverend decided to choose twelve girls, all approximately eleven years old, to form a fledgling group of pipers that would become known as The Dagenham Girl Pipers. He could not have imagined how popular and important these girls would become to the people of Essex. During his lifetime, he was able to see the potential of the group he had created in 1930. He would surely be proud to know that his girls are still performing throughout the world decked out in their Royal Stuart kilts, jackets and sporrans. Perhaps, after seeing the girls perform on television or in a documentary, he would proudly announce as many still do today, 'They're from Dagenham you know.'

The Dagenham Girl Pipers. (Peggy Iris)

Peggy Iris was one of the first twelve girls chosen from Reverend Graves' Sunday school group that made up the original Dagenham Girl Pipers. She fondly remembers how the group entertained our troops during the Second World War as part of ENSA (Entertainments National Service Association) and brought some special cheer at Christmas gatherings:

> I was just eleven years old when I was chosen as one of the original twelve Dagenham Girl Pipers by Reverend Graves. I remember the training was quite hard but it all depended on the individual,

her keenness to learn as to how quickly she was assimilated into the group. Usually, one can get familiar with the pipes in about six months, but we had to practise very hard every day to get proficient. My pipes came from Scotland and were made by James Robertson of Edinburgh – after a while, they became part of me.

Over the years, the group grew in size to approximately seventy to eighty girls although we didn't all appear at the same time. It all depended on the venue and what kind of event. There could be as few as two girls or as many as forty, it just depended on what was needed. I would say that an average of sixteen girls would appear at any one time.

We were rarely home at Christmas and the New Year because of our demanding schedule. There was always a pantomime to attend or some other function that could be half way around the world. I don't recall any special songs that we sang so long as we included Scotland the Brave, which always seemed to appeal to everyone.

I have had a wonderful life; have met so many people who have become my friends. I have never regretted that day when Reverend Graves picked me as an eleven-year-old to be one of 'the twelve'. I'm proud that the Dagenham Girl Pipers became and still are such a wonderful success.

I was asked to start a girl's piping band in Singapore and when I arrived was told that six months was all we had to train the girls for a special event. They were a grand bunch of girls and learned quickly, practising non stop. Six months later they marched before the Singapore Government and a huge crowd. They were brilliant.

I try to get to the annual reunions, meet old friends and it is wonderful to reminisce about past times, the people we met and find out how our colleagues are getting on in different parts of the world. Alas, time passes and our numbers seem to diminish with each year.

A Postman's Life

The lead-up to the Christmas holidays has always been particularly hard on our postal service and especially our postmen who have to contend with the extra post. Jack Bartlett, a postman for over thirty-five years and who is now ninety-two years old, vividly recalls what life was like in the early 1900s. As an adult, he became a postman, a job he loved all his life. He has seen tremendous changes in the postal service from when letters and packages were hand stamped and delivered by bicycle, to an automated service and delivery by vans:

> As a boy, I recall my mother used to begin getting ready for Christmas in September by making the Christmas pudding, sometimes making an extra pudding to keep for the following year. We also used to make sloe wine which was made in the old country tradition of collecting the sloes as soon as they had seen the first frost.
>
> I remember that I didn't like school much as a child and was known to run away. One day, I ran all the way home. The journey was about a mile, which was a long way for a five year old. When I got home, my mother sent me all the way back to school, so I never did that again!
>
> When I grew up I became a postman. We wore navy blue wool uniforms in the winter and lighter weight uniforms in the summer. We used to get into trouble if we didn't keep our caps on. We worked long shifts and usually worked a forty-eight-hour week. On regular days, I used to get up at 3.30 a.m. to begin work at 4.15 a.m., but even

A postman's life. (Jack Bartlett)

that wasn't good enough over the Christmas holidays to keep up with the extra post. In 1949, there were no automatic franking machines, so everything had to be hand stamped. We used to stamp about 55,000 items a day. Of course, we couldn't go home until our work was done, so that meant I got home very late on Christmas day which didn't please my wife one bit! We used to make two deliveries each day (including Christmas Day) so I used have my Christmas dinner at around 2.00 p.m. which was in between deliveries. Sometimes, I was so tired I went to sleep over my dinner! Also, we had to deal with the turkeys that arrived on Christmas Eve. These weighed over 10lbs each, so they were hard to deal with on top of the extra post.

Delivering the post in those days was not easy as some of the roads were still unmade. The weather played a big part of the job too – sometimes it was good and other times it was horrible especially when the roads were icy or we'd had a storm like we did in 1953. That time was really bad as I had to manoeuvre around fallen trees, branches and flooded roads. I had all of this to contend with as well as having my deliveries piled up on my bike. All that post made my bike really heavy to handle, so the job was quite dangerous at times. Still, I did my rounds and people were amazed that I was able to deliver the post on time even in bad weather. Mrs Emery, a postmistress once told me that instead of blood, I had postal ink in my veins – I think I have to agree with her.

Celebrations at Oldchurch Hospital

There are few institutions in Essex that are more fondly remembered than Oldchurch Hospital. For almost 165 years, literally hundreds of thousands have passed through its doors as the staff welcomed new babies into the world, repaired broken bones and rehabilitated patients. Unfortunately, this wonderful old building is being replaced by a new and vibrant hospital called Queen's Hospital that replaces the old.

The following extracts are from a book titled *A Brief History of Oldchurch Hospital* by Queenie M. Jackson. The book is dedicated

to two distinguished matrons, Miss E.M. McArthur and Miss N. Howley:

> In 1839 Romford Union Workhouse was designed by Francis Edwards and built for the cost of £8,709 on a two-and-a-half-acre site of open farmland. It was the only building in Oldchurch Road, Romford. It was administered by a Board of Guardians.
>
> The workhouse was built in a square with buildings on each side. In the centre was a cruciform block. The tailor's shop and boot store were in a separate building, as were the kitchen and dining room but both were within the workhouse complex.
>
> The workhouse contained a female infirm ward, a male infirm ward, casual wards for vagrants, female and male observation wards, male and female day rooms and dormitories for 'inmates'. Romford Union Lying-in Ward 1857 Bible was found and so confirms the workhouse had a maternity ward.
>
> The workhouse had its own carpenters, plumbers, and barbers shops and general stores. It also contained matron's office and staff residential accommodation. The matron's and master's accommodation was centrally placed and nearest to the kitchen.
>
> There was overnight accommodation for vagrants. The casuals needing accommodation for the night were searched to make sure they were genuinely penniless.
>
> The infirmary was built in 1893. It was an H-shaped building with administrative offices in the middle and the maternity ward above (top office to generations of nurses) at each side were ward block (A and B).
>
> In 1924 the stone was laid for the Nurses Home. The building contained a main entrance, sitting rooms, dining rooms, kitchen, bedroom

Celebrations at Oldchurch Hospital. (Oldchurch Hospital Archives)

block 7 and 8. Block 6 was added in 1929. C Ward Block and D Ward Block were built in 1924.

The hospital nursed military personnel from the First and Second World Wars and even nursed enemy servicemen. Over the years, departments were enlarged and others formed.

The 1970s saw changes in nurse training. The Romford School of Nursing was formed in 1971 by the amalgamation of the separate Schools of Nursing and by 1974 the last Oldchurch trainees had completed their training. The hospital badge was altered to the Romford School of Nursing. Two year later the Area School of Nursing was formed joining the Romford, Brentwood and Warley Schools of Nursing.

In 1973 a further phase of the hospital development occurred and B Block was demolished to make way for a sixty-bedded Neurosurgical

Centre. The X-ray Department and telephone exchange were part of this development phrase.

The Barking and Havering Area Health Authority, the Romford Area Health Authority and the Romford District Management Team took over management responsibility from the Romford Hospital Management Committee in 1974. The old Out Patients' department opened in the 1930s was converted into an E.C.N. centre.

Sadly in 1975 the hospital chapel built in 1839 was destroyed by fire. In 1976 the hospital chapel, canteen, kitchens, boiler house and Occupational Therapy extensions were built.

Theresa Francis, now Therapy Head of Service, recalls life at Oldchurch Hospital in the early 1970s when she was a young occupational therapist:

Celebrations at Oldchurch Hospital. (Oldchurch Hospital 1950s, Mrs Joyce Burgess)

Christmas was obviously a difficult time for the patients to be away from their families, but we tried to do all we could to make the wards and departments as festive as possible. The occupational therapists would decide on a special 'theme' to decorate their department. I remember that one year there was a Chinese theme; another was floral, and so on. On Christmas Eve, some members of the staff used to go from ward to ward singing carols – I enjoyed that very much. Nurses and therapists would take the patients into the chapel for a carol service and then return to the Occupational Therapy Department for a little celebration with mince pies and a beverage. I don't recall ever seeing one of our physicians carving the turkey at Christmas dinner during the 1970s but I've heard from nurses at other hospitals that this was done back in the 1950s. In fact, I think I remember seeing a photograph of a physician carving a turkey at Christmas at Harold Wood Hospital. All in all, we tried our best to make our patients as comfortable and as happy possible. They seemed to enjoy and appreciate our efforts.

A Physician's Family

Sybil Watt of Hornchurch remembers when Christmas Day meant duty, responsibility and a personal desire to make the day special for the patients in her husband's care. Dr John Watt (now sadly departed) began his life as the house officer at Oldchurch Hospital, Romford, and finished his career as a consultant.

Dr Watt and his wife, Sybil, both originally from Scotland, married in 1940 and moved soon after to Essex where the doctor began his profession at Oldchurch Hospital. These were happy but hard years for a young, conscientious physician with a growing family. It was the second year of the Second World War, and although the general feeling of the people were optimistic about the outcome of the war, the years during and after were exceptionally difficult. Many items were on ration and some were simply not available.

Sybil Watt recalls what Christmas Day was like for her own family forty to fifty years ago. As the wife of a dedicated physician, she enjoyed helping the less fortunate, especially those in hospital:

> In the 1940s and 1950s, nursing staff gave their lives to the hospital and the care of their patients. At special times such as Christmas, the effort was doubled as each ward was decorated and had a huge tree. A small gift was found for every patient – even during wartime. Even new babies' cots had a tiny decoration placed on them – nobody was forgotten!
>
> The senior staff member for each ward, usually the consultant, would arrive at the hospital around midday to carve the turkey and then return to their families. At around 3.30 p.m. all the medical staff and their families toured the wards in their care, talked to each patient, and handed each one a small present taken from the tree. This was something I particularly enjoyed and it gave me great pleasure to distribute the gifts. Some medical staff members toured other wards as well as their own, but everyone visited the children's ward. The hospital's choir, which consisted mostly of administrative staff, toured the wards singing carols. After this, the medical staff and families socialised in the ward annexe.

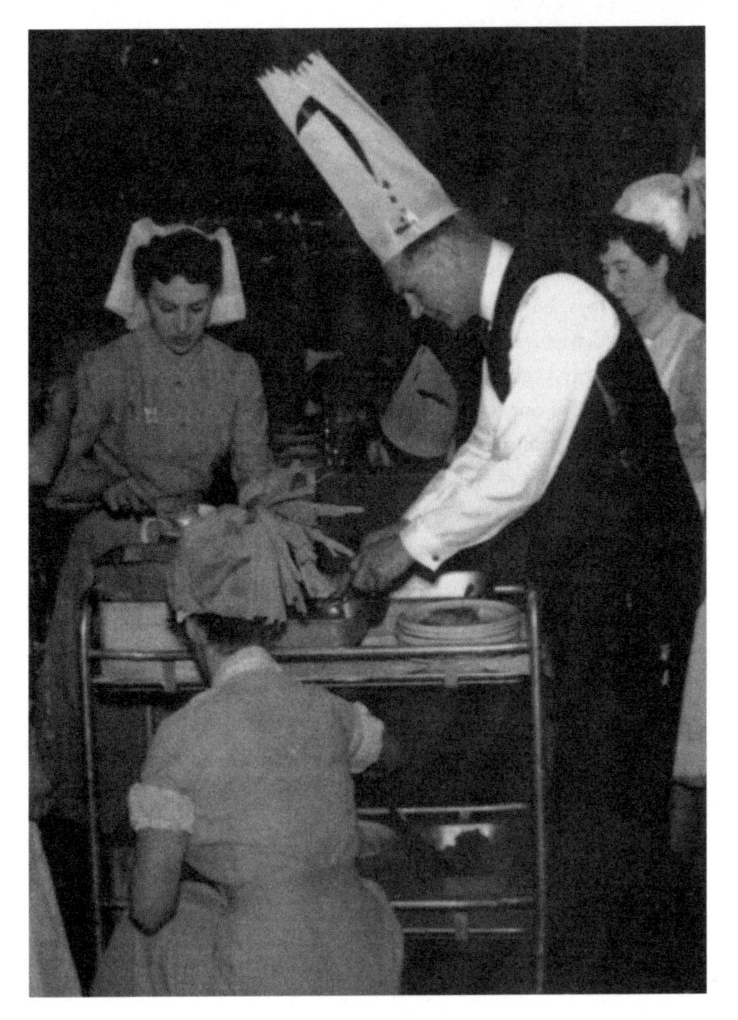

A physician's family. (Harold Wood Hospital 1950s, Miss Eileen Ward)

When I look back at those years, it was hard to have a traditional Christmas Day in our own household. John and I used to enjoy watching the children open their presents and then we would have our breakfast. At midday, John would leave to go to the hospital to carve the turkey and then return home. In the meantime, I used to get the children's clothes laid out in readiness for our afternoon visit to the hospital. Of course, the children never liked to leave their newly acquired toys, but by laying their clothes out, it meant for a quick and easy departure. Since we are a Scottish family, I recall one year when I wanted the boys to wear their traditional kilts and shirts, so laid those items out on their beds. Imagine my horror when I noticed our family dachshund had obviously been on the boys' bed because their outfits were covered in dog hairs! It was a hairy mess, and I had to spend considerable time brushing the boys' clothes to make them look respectable before we could leave for the hospital.

I suppose, we really celebrated our Christmas Day on Boxing Day – at least that's when we had a proper Christmas dinner. We often visited John's aunt and uncle who had a farm in North Weald. John's aunt used to cook on an Aga stove which made the whole kitchen warm and welcoming. I remember that it was a wonderful treat to enjoy a nice meal after such a hectic day the day before – but it was worth the effort because it gave us all pleasure and I know it brought joy to the patients.

The Workhouse

Many people in Essex during the 1850s lived from hand-to-mouth, basically surviving on a pittance. Should the primary provider become too ill to work, or worse yet die, the family would become destitute. Many times, extended family members came to their aid, but in some instances, the only recourse was the workhouse.

In 1719, just such a workhouse was built close to Sun Corner in Billericay and later in 1840 the Billericay Union Workhouse was built at the cost of £11,000. The workhouse was built on an 11-acre plot and was located between Norsey and Stock Roads.

In 1834, the Poor Law Act was introduced in England. As result of this act, groups of parishes joined together to form unions so that rates could be levied for the purpose of funding local workhouses.

The following extract is courtesy of the *Weekly News* and Sylvia Kent:

> The 11-acre plot of land for the new workhouse lay between Stock and Norsey Roads. It served 26 parishes including Brentwood and was even mentioned favourably by George Orwell in his classic novel, *Down and Out in London and Paris.*
>
> The late Mary Needham, born in 1908, was one of the daughters of the last master and matron of the Union Workhouse.
>
> During the final years of her long life, Mary gave many talks about her childhood at her workhouse home.

'I have vivid recollections of the workhouse, which was built by Sir George Gilbert Scott in 1840,' she said. 'The main entrance was in Norsey Road, where the porter's lodge still exists and there was another entrance in Stock Road. Lovely red bricks were used and indigo-blue bricks formed a fascinating diamond pattern.

There was a chapel for inmates, which still exists and they did attend regularly. A hospital was added in 1897, with 44 beds. Much later, this became St Andrew's – famous for its Burns Unit.'

Mary remembered Christmas as a special time in the workhouse. 'My parents and staff did their best to make this a happy occasion for everyone,' she said.

'The Board of Guardians gave mother a lump sum with which to buy gifts for the children. Miss Wade, near the church and Mrs. Stammers in Billericay High Street supplied the toys. Cook mixed the Christmas puddings in a big wooden trough and cooked them in her huge steamers in the kitchen. The pigs, which had been carefully fed throughout the year under my father's instructions, were killed in readiness for the Christmas dinner. Every year, Mr. Heseltine, the guardian from Great Warley, sent a bottle of sweets for each child and Billericay shopkeepers contributed food and gifts. When Christmas day dawned, there was an extra half-ounce of tobacco and beer for the men and ginger-beer and sweets for the women and children.

My father, Walter Needham and Dr Wells, the medical superintendent, carved the huge joints of pork, served with home-grown vegetables and followed by large portions of Christmas pudding,' Mary recalls.

Mary went on to become a schoolteacher and returned to Billericay to live the rest of her days in sheltered accommodation opposite her

old home, by then the St Andrews Hospital. It was later demolished when the Burns Unit was moved to Broomfield.

A Christmas Wedding

Mary Margaret Hall married Martin Ambrose Bray on Christmas Day, 1930. The decision to marry on Christmas Day may have been made for practical reasons as Reverend Elwin Cockett recalls:

> Researching my family tree, I discovered that a number of my ancestors were married on Christmas day, albeit mostly in the early nineteenth century. It is very rare these days and, in fact, I have *never* taken a wedding on Christmas Day. I suspect that it was more common in the past because Christmas Day was a universal holiday, which meant that the couple and their friends would be off work.

Mary and Martin began their life together first in London where two of their five daughters, Margaret, and Evelyn, were born. Their third daughter, Sylvia was born in Hitchin, Hertfordshire, and the last two girls; Shirley and Betty were born in Dagenham, Essex, to where the family had moved in 1942.

The eldest girl, Margaret reminisces:

> The lead-up to Christmas was almost as exciting as Christmas itself. The Christmas puddings and cake would be made weeks before

A Christmas wedding. (Mr and Mrs Martin Bray)

Christmas and put away in the larder. But before the mixture was put in the pudding basins, our mother followed a tradition that perhaps had been part of her childhood. Each member of the family took turns with the wooden spoon and stirred the mixture three times in a clockwise direction as they made a wish. The spoon was then passed to the next person and the next, until all members of the family had fulfilled their solemn duty of stirring the pudding three times in a clockwise direction. When this was done, a silver Joey, a three-penny bit, was added to the pudding mixture, the lucky member of the fam-

A Christmas wedding.
(Mr and Mrs Martin Bray)

ily who was served the pudding containing the Joey could expect much wealth throughout the New Year.

Evelyn remembers that many items were still on ration after the Second World War:

Mum or dad used to take our ration books and say, 'We need to save those for Christmas'. We used to hear that expression quite a lot 'saving it for Christmas'. In fact, one year, I had been taken to hospital

with appendicitis and was evidently quite poorly. I remember though seeing a large Christmas tree in the ward and thought, 'Goody, I'll get another Christmas present'. Unfortunately, it didn't work out that way. I developed pneumonia after the operation, and was sent away to convalesce in Clacton for several months. I remember missing my family dreadfully, but dad used to visit me after doing a stint of night work in London. Bless his heart; he would arrive with his pockets full of sweets and comics. The sweets were taken away by the matron who then shared them with all the other children. I didn't like that very much, didn't think it was fair.

Sylvia actually remembers the ambulance taking her sister Evelyn away:

I remember when Eve was taken to hospital because we were staying at our Aunt Liz's home in East Ham, and I cried because I couldn't see into the blackened ambulance windows, and was scared for my sister. I must have only been about four or five years of age but remember that she was taken to Whipps Cross Hospital, Leytonstone. We visited her in hospital and gave her some chocolates – such a luxury in those days.

For Christmas dinner, we usually had a chicken that dad killed and then perhaps a rabbit for Boxing Day. Since everything was in short supply after the war, mum made a kind of funny marzipan that was in fact made from Soya flour – heavily dosed with almond essence. We used to make paper chains using coloured strips of paper. The strips came in thin packets and we linked the chains with flour paste that was very mucky. Once the chains were made the whole living room would be draped with them plus a good dose of silver tinsel, masses of

it. We used to listen to the Christmas message from the King on the radio until about 1953 when Queen Elizabeth came to the throne.

Shirley, the fourth daughter in the family, reminisces:

Dad would go 'all out' to provide us with loads of fruit, nuts and sweets. It was all so exciting as we had so little during the year, this was like a huge bonanza – wonderful and so different, which is why I loved Christmas. We didn't have many toys because there was little money for that kind of thing. Mum and dad used to put 6d or 1s a week into a Christmas fund at the Working Men's Club down at the Trades Hall. The Trades Hall was in Charlotte Road close to the Old Dagenham Village. Sometime in December, mum and dad would collect their savings that had all been dutifully recorded throughout the year, and splurge it on all on Christmas. I recall too that we used to sing a little ditty on Christmas Eve as we went to bed. I wonder how many other families sang the same song, 'As we climb the stairs, with our sleepy heads, hang our stockings up … hang them in a row.' What a pleasant memory – what fun we had!

Betty, the youngest of the five Bray sisters, wonders if some of the customs and traditions were brought from London:

Since mum and dad were originally from London, I've often wondered if other families in Essex had the same traditions. I remember that my favourite part of Christmas was finding my stocking at the end of my bed and knowing that Santa had come in the night. There would always be some fruit and nuts in the stocking and other little items such as chocolate coins wrapped in gold foil, but the thing I enjoyed the

most was dancing around the Christmas tree. The tree was obviously not very tall but it must have seemed very tall to me as a young child. Anyhow, after the tree was placed on the floor in the centre of the living room, we sisters linked hands and danced around the tree chanting, 'Who shall we get to pick the tree, pick the tree, pick the tree, on this cold and frosty morning?' A chosen member of the family, (usually the eldest) would step forward and take something off the tree, a sweet or small trinket and then the song was repeated until every person had had a 'turn.' As I was the 'baby' of the family, I always got the fairy off the tree which was a real treat. Most of the items that were on the tree were tiny things that were probably bought at the Woolworth's shop in the Heathway – it didn't matter, they were special to us.

Christmas Tree Farm

The Fred Smith Christmas Tree Farm at Boxted near Colchester has been growing Christmas trees since 1961. The business began when a friend of Fred's gave him a few Christmas trees and, as they grew in size, so did a fledging business. Nowadays, the farm provides trees not only for private use, but also in the commercial sector too. Tim Smith, second generation says:

> We offer an old fashioned, personal service to our customers. We take the time to discuss our customers' needs, what kind of tree they'd

Christmas Tree Farm.
(Mr and Mrs Smith)

prefer and we'll even dig it up and prepare it for delivery if they wish. Some people like to dig their own trees, usually between 6-7ft feet as their children or grandchildren are standing by. They may even video the event especially if the couple has a new child and want to record their child's first Christmas tree. Our customers return every year – one lady has been coming back to us every year for thirty-five years! That's quite a record.

Tim Smith notes:

> The Norway spruce is probably the favourite tree in our inventory, but we also supply blue spruce and Nordmann fir. The holly used in the wreaths is all grown locally and is of exceptional quality. Our wreaths are made to order and we all help in producing them. We pride ourselves on our personal service and expertise to our customers. Our motto is 'trees for all, small or tall'.

Helping Santa

Crossing patrol officer or the 'lollypop lady' as she is affectionately known by the children she helps daily, Doreen Waters happily accepts both titles. She loves her job and enjoys seeing and talking to the children every day as she escorts them across the road. But their lives are very different from Doreen's own childhood, when she went to live at Hutton Poplars Residential School.

The memories of those times are still very close to Doreen's heart, especially those from the Christmas holidays because it was such an important time for all the children living in the orphanage. One Christmas, when Doreen was about five years old, she was photographed with a girl (now unknown) as they held a mirror for the headmaster, Mr Higdon, who was carefully fixing his eyebrows on with glue in preparation for his for his role as Santa Claus. Doreen still remembers that special Christmas:

Helping Santa.
(Doreen Waters)

My brother and I went to live at the home I suppose because our mother couldn't support us. I don't remember being sad or unhappy while I lived there but I do remember how excited we all were when Christmas came. As you can see from this photograph, Mr Higdon participated in the celebrations and became Santa for a day. You know, I remember that dress I am wearing in the photograph! There was so much starch in that collar that in rubbed my neck sore. You can see how the little collar is standing up – it was so stiff!

There were about 600 boys and girls at the home although the boys and girls were kept separate for the most part. We were kept in blocks, I lived in Block 9, still remember it to this day. We called the women who took care of us 'nurses' not 'teachers'.

Mr Higdon particularly liked the children to participate in all sorts of theatrical activities such as plays, but most of all he liked us to perform in a pantomime held on Boxing Day – we had a nice stage at the school that even had a trap door!

I stayed at the home until I was about fourteen years and six months but then my mother wanted me back home. I did return as my mother wished, but her home was so cramped I had to share a bed with my sister Margaret who was a year and a half older than me. I so much wanted to return to the Poplars School and have my own bed again. One day, my sister took me to see my grandmother whom I had never met but who regularly sent me a 6d when I lived at the Poplars. She sewed the 6d into a kind of little pouch. Also in the pouch was a two-and-a-half-penny stamp which I used on an envelope to send her a letter of thanks. Anyway, I was a little nervous of meeting my grandmother after all these years but the meeting went all right. I recall that my grandmother was dressed completely in black with button-up black boots, her white hair pulled into a bun at the back of her head.

Eventually, I did return to the Poplars School, but the job I had been promised as matron's maid to Matron Knight had been taken by another girl. I had no regrets of losing the job because the young girl who took it had had a more difficult life than my own, having been deserted as a newborn baby.

All in all, I had a wonderful life and have no regrets about being raised at the Poplars School. The staff did a grand job especially at Christmas time and tried their best to make it a happy time for all

the children. We particularly used to look forward to the presents that would be sent by people who donated them to *The Evening News* and from other publications. So on the whole, I have no regrets, and my young life was a happy one.

James Merriott's Essex

Born in the East End of London in 1941, James Merriott remembers life as a very young child when he was evacuated to the village of Brent Eleigh in Suffolk during the Second World War. After the war ended, he returned to his home in Poplar with his brother and three sisters. As so many families did during the war, James's parents stayed behind in London but sent their children to the relative safety of the countryside until the war ended.

In 1967, James married his wife Joan, and settled in Brentwood where they have remained to this day. He loves the countryside of Essex with a passion that can be seen in his beautiful watercolour paintings. It appears that almost every scene in Essex has been blessed with a rendition of James' work, from Colchester Castle to Thaxted Windmill, and so many more. He considers every sunny day in the countryside a true 'Christmas gift' and one that he takes advantage of by painting a specific scene with the speed and proficiency necessary to capture the light and beauty of his subject. In fact James has always regarded himself as a 'countryman':

James Merriott's Essex. (James Merriott)

Like most children of my age, life had its ups and downs but we were no different from most of the people in my neighbourhood. The men went to work each day, and the women stayed home to take care of their families.

My earliest recollections of drawing were during my infant school years where the teacher had given us an assignment of drawing the altar in our school. Bearing in mind, we were only about five-years-old, so to be asked to draw the altar was quite a challenge. However, since drawing had always come naturally to me, I was able to produce a good likeness and the teacher was so pleased with my efforts that she had me display my drawing to the whole school.

After passing the eleven-plus I attended St Bernard's Roman Catholic School in Stepney, East London. It was a very strict and disciplined school but it was here that the teachers encouraged me to draw and explore my talent. On reflection, I suppose I already knew the basic drawing techniques because it had been taught to me at home. Art had always been a big part of our family's activities and interest. In fact, my uncle Jack Merriott (1901-1968), had been the vice president of the Royal Institute of Painters in Watercolours – so you could say that painting is in my family's blood.

My earliest recollection of Christmas was when I was about eight years old and I desperately wanted an electric train set. Dad was a 'radio wizard' in the days of wireless, and so he was able to rig up a microphone which enabled me to send my wishes directly to 'Santa'. I must admit, I was completely taken in and didn't realise until much later that 'Santa' had been my own dad! I remember being absolutely thrilled that I had received the very present that I had asked 'Santa' to bring. The special train set made that Christmas one of my all time favourites.

Although we did play games during the day, Christmas dinner was always the highlight of the holiday. My mum was no different from all the other mums who wanted to prepare a special Christmas dinner for their families. We always had a good dinner and pudding, but of course some things were difficult, if not impossible, to get. During the war and even post war, many items were on strict ration, but still mum managed to put a nice meal on the table.

Mum and dad always encouraged me to be active and participate in all the boyhood activities including the cubs and later the scouts, but some of my most memorable experiences were riding through the Essex countryside on my sister's hand-me-down bike. I think this made me aware of my surroundings and has helped me appreciate the

James Merriott's Essex. (James Merriott)

beauty that is all around me. Many of the scenes depicted in my paintings I first saw as a child, some during the summer and others during the winter. I can't remember too many white Christmases, although there was one in 1947 when we seemed to have snow on the ground almost every day. The weather didn't necessarily stop us from doing anything outside and, when I reflect back, those days in the countryside – rain or sun, were some of the happiest of my childhood.

I suppose my experiences in those early years all led to my love of painting. One of the things I love most is the beauty of the white paper; I try, to the best of my ability, to achieve transparency and purity in my paintings which is why I have always loved painting snow.

Romford Market

Many people may recall going to Romford Market on Christmas Eve for those last minute gift items but also for the special deals that could be had in the form of a nice capon, turkey or other fowl for Christmas dinner. The stall holders knew only too well there would be a rush on this final day before Christmas and were well prepared to sell their merchandise or risk being left with unwanted produce.

Clara Hall, a resident of Dagenham recalls how years ago, her family took advantage of those special bargains in Romford Market:

> Just after the war, things were very difficult especially at Christmas when parents wanted to do something nice for their families, but money was always tight and especially so at Christmas. But many families like ours saved money each week in a working men's club. My parents used to save 6d or 1s each week, which was a lot of money in those days, and then draw out the funds at the end of the year. This way, we always had some extra money to spend at Christmas time. We knew from past years that bargains could be had at Romford Market if we waited until the last minute. We knew the stall holders would 'do a deal' because they didn't want anything left on their stalls at the end of the day, so it was in their best interest to sell everything off at bargain prices, especially the turkeys and other birds because they could 'go off'. Of course, there was no refrigeration, the birds used to hang around the top of the stall on hooks or would be laid out on the

Romford Market. (Private collection)

bed of the stall. There were capons, turkeys, ducks and geese and even the odd rabbit for sale, so if you were willing to make the effort to get to the market, a bargain could be had.

I remember the atmosphere of the people waiting on the Heathway bundled up against the cold for a number 175 or a 174 bus that would take us almost to the market. Once there, the foot traffic would be so great that we would come to a complete standstill due to the sheer volume of people. But it was the noise and smell of the market that seemed to excite the people. I remember as a child that, as we walked past a certain stall, a man or woman would call out and I would remember that person from one year to the next because of their distinctive voice or speech pattern. Many stall holders would have a

'barker', a person who would entice a passer-by with the promise of a 'special'. Once 'hooked', the individual, especially if it was a woman, would be treated to personal compliments from the stall holder, 'You look lovely today darling, what a nice coat you've got on? Do you want this 10-lb turkey, it's nice and juicy … you can have it for … not £5 … not £4 ... but it's yours for only £2 10 shillings!' A nod from the spectator in the nice coat as an acceptance and the stall holder would clap his hands, and a deal was done, just like that!

The Christmas bird wasn't the only bargain that could be had; nuts, dates, figs and tangerines were available if you had the money. Other stalls specialised in vegetables, cheeses, and sweets and yet other stalls catered towards gifts for the family.

Then came the rush back home holding our own canvas or plastic bags – there were no polythene bags given to us in those days as the stall holder would slide the veggies or fruit directly off the scales into our bags. I remember how heavy those bags used to be as we trekked back to the bus stop – but then, we had to make the trip worth the expense. When the bus finally arrived, it was often full on the lower level and the conductor would say 'only room up top love' and so we would struggle with our bags up the spiral steps and then collapse in laughter once we'd sat down.

The big treat for me was to have a drink on the way home from Romford market in the Church Elm Pub in the Heathway. Mum and dad would have a drink and buy me a bottle of lemonade and a bag of crisps. In those days, the crisps were not salted but instead the salt was inside the bag in a small twist of blue, waxed paper. I always liked to open the paper and sprinkle the salt into the crisps all by myself and shake the bag – isn't it funny the things we remember?

Special Little Horses

The pleasure of seeing two Falabella horses dressed in special outfits is enough to bring a smile to anyone's face at the best of times, but especially at Christmas. Seen here with their young host at a charita-

Special little horses. (Sylvia Kent)

ble Christmas event are two Falabellas, one of whom is pregnant.

An Essex stud farm provides these exceptional horses for charitable events that include raising money for Little Haven's Hospice, MacMillan Nurses and Schools for Disabled Children.

The horses are sure to raise the spirits of all those with whom they come into contact, especially children. The Falabella horse is gregarious but gentle in nature and, with their silky manes and soft skin, they invite the petting which they seem to enjoy.

The Falabella horse is believed to have originated in Argentina where, during the middle of the nineteenth century, the family of Falabella kept a herd and through selective breeding maintained the same proportions and temperament of the breed. The horses are usually black or brown but sometimes the colour may vary from pinto, to bay or chestnut. They are extremely long-lived with a life span of forty to fifty years.

Town Crier and Toastmaster

Jim Shrubb, town crier of Billericay and Toastmaster, brings a special touch to any occasion whether he officiates at a charity ball, wedding or Christmas event. When Jim appears in his town crier's bright red jacket, cape, tricorne-feathered hat, buckled shoes, black breeches and white stockings; the audience knows they are in for a treat. Likewise, when he dons his toastmaster's outfit of hunting pink

Town crier and toastmaster. (James Shrubb)

tailcoat, black high-waisted dress trousers, with twin braid down the seams and carrying his gavel, the spectators are anxious to hear Jim speak and enjoy the event. His repertoire varies depending on the venue, but typically a civic or charitable event may require a more formal presentation. During these times, Jim ceremoniously opens a scroll and reads aloud a specific message. This tradition of addressing an audience originated when most people in England could neither read nor write, therefore it was necessary for the reigning monarch or other dignitary to have a designated speaker, someone who could go into the street and make announcements.

Jim's appearance is guaranteed to get peoples' attention whether at a Christmas lighting ceremony or escorting Santa through the market-place. But he does hold one item close to his heart – his precious bell. The bell was a gift from his Uncle Charlie who, at the age of ninety years, purchased the bell at the Whitechapel Bell Foundry. The bell is an important part of Jim's ensemble, not only because it was a special gift from a favourite uncle, but because it bears an inscription to Charlie's wife, Frances. This makes the bell all the more precious and gives him pleasure each time it is rung.

Born in London, Jim married his wife Sue on 26 March 1977 and moved to Billericay following their wedding and honeymoon; they have lived in Billericay since then and have five wonderful children ranging in age from thirteen to twenty-eight years. They are very active in local community events especially their church, Emmanuel, built on the site of the Old Archer Hall:

> Christmas is special for me because I am a committed Christian. Together with my wife and family members, we usually attend several Christmas services including the Christingle service, the midnight communion on Christmas Eve, and sometimes the Christmas morning service as well. I have had the privilege of reading out a proclamation in a number of churches in the area. I believe the Arch Angel Gabriel was one of the earliest town criers or messengers with his 'Fear not, I bring tidings of great joy ...' I also organise a 20-ft high Christmas tree for our church each year which is turned into a Holy cross for Easter, an idea my wife Sue founded.
>
> My life as a town crier and toastmaster is kept very busy year round because I also appear in many other counties such as Kent, Sussex, Hertfordshire and Norfolk, just to mention a few. However, I would say

Town crier and toastmaster. (James Shrubb)

> the majority of my events are here in Essex. You know, one of the most enjoyable parts of my job is that I make people smile – that's a great accomplishment for me. To see happy, enthusiastic people enjoying themselves at a function that I am attending … well, that brings me great joy!

Growing up in London, Jim has maintained a close relationship with several of his oldest friends from Manor Park. Some describe him as 'a man of many talents' and of 'having a great heart'. These comments explain why Jim is in such great demand both as a town crier and a toastmaster.

The 'Mad' Maldon Mud Race

The Maldon Mud Race began as a simple wager over thirty years ago, but has developed into an event that raises thousands of pounds for local charities and is now featured on international television. The race is organised by the International Lions and Rotary Clubs of Maldon, supported by Maldon District Council and sponsored by Asheldam Feed Centre.

The following extract on the origin of the race is from the International Lions and Rotary Clubs of Maldon:

> The 'race' originated in 1973, with a dare being given by a local resident to the landlord of the Queen's Head public house, which stands on Hythe Quay in Maldon, Essex, challenging him to serve a meal on the salting of the river Blackwater whilst dressed in a tuxedo. The challenge was fully accepted and carried out, resulting in the next year a bar being opened on the saltings. About twenty people made a mad dash across the river bed, drank a pint of beer and dashed back; this was the beginning of the Maldon Mud Race. In subsequent years so many people wished to take part in the event that the time taken to consume the beer caused a 'logjam' on the saltings, so that part of the event was discontinued and reverted to a dash over the river bed and back again.

The race has even been linked to an invasion by the Danes. In 991, Britnoth, an Anglo-Saxon leader rallied the men of Maldon to fight the

The 'Mad' Maldon Mud Race. (Sylvia Kent)

Danes and defend their village. The Danes, unfamiliar with the depth of the mud in the Blackwater, became stranded on the mudflats and requested that Britnoth, in fair play, allow them to reassemble their men on firm ground before battle. A valiant man, Britnoth agreed to this request, but it proved a fatal strategic blunder. The Danes won the battle and Britnoth literally lost his head. Some say the head was taken by the Danes as a trophy of battle, while others believe that Britnoth's skull is still to be found in the muddy depths of the river. To this end, a romantic legend has developed among some of the participants of the race that perhaps one of them will discover the head of their Saxon leader.

Martin Wood, 'Mad' Maldon Mud Race treasurer, said:

> The International Lions and Rotary Clubs decided to restart the race in 2001. For years the race had been stymied because of one reason or

> the other, but once we got it going, it has grown and become more popular and successful each year. We are pleased to announce that we were able to present £27,000 that was distributed to local charities from the 2006 race.

On 31 December 2006, hundreds of people joined the race dressed in fantastic costumes ranging from Santa outfits to cocktail waitresses and everything in between. Much fun was had by all, especially the spectators. The event was even broadcast on international news channels. From the hundreds who participated, the first three to cross the

The 'Mad' Maldon Mud Race. (Sylvia Kent)

finish line were Richard Weston, first, Mark Bailey, second and Kevin Mason, third place.

Nowadays, almost twenty teams join the race with creative names such as the 'Mud Monsters', 'The Mud, the Bad and the Ugly' and the 'Muddy, Muddy Marksmen'. In 2006, the first three places were awarded to '3 Westons & Friend' – first, the 'Lost Boys' – second and the 'Dirty Half Dozen' – third.

Victorian Evening

Newly appointed councillor Tony Cussen of Bradwell-on-Sea looks back at his life growing up in London before his family, like so many others, moved across the border to Essex. Now councillor Cussen administers to four parishes, Althorne, Latchingdon, Mundon and Maylandsea as part of his duties.

> Growing up in London was a lot different to my life in rural Essex but it was still a lot of fun. My grandparents lived with us on the ground floor of a huge Victorian house, so there was always a lot of activity in our home especially during the Christmas holidays. I remember my sister Kim and I were always too excited to go to sleep on Christmas Eve, and tried in vain to stay awake in the hopes of catching Santa, but we never did and sleep got the better of us. We still managed to wake at the crack of dawn! I do remember having some great toys such as

a Beatles guitar – that was a completely unexpected gift and one that I really enjoyed. I spent many hours strutting around the house singing and strumming away like one of my heroes. I couldn't play it of course and it was to be some thirty seven years later that I would pick up a guitar and play for real. Another year, I received a ten shilling note from my grandma which really surprised me too. Fifty pence is not much in today's money but was a considerable sum in those days which you could use to buy all sorts of toys.

Christmas dinner was traditional in the sense we had turkey, stuffing, roast potatoes and vegetables and of course the table was decorated with Christmas crackers. Mum, dad and our grandparents all made us stand up when the Queen gave her Christmas message – all in all, we used to have a good time.

We tried to continue those traditions with our own children and hope in turn they will do likewise with their own children. My wife Susan, on Christmas Eve would meticulously place the empty stockings at the foot of the children's bed, where they would wake, in the morning to find them full of presents to a cry of, 'He's been he's been, Santa's been!' There was also half a glass of milk and a half eaten biscuit next to the fireplace where we'd placed them on Christmas Eve. Santa had obviously refreshed himself before continuing his onward journey! Next Christmas, I'm certain that my son Ross and his wife Vicki will be doing the same for our first and newly arrived granddaughter, Lexi Elizabeth. That's what it's all about, continuity!

My plan is to continue the good work in Maldon that my predecessor, Michael Helm and others have worked so hard to maintain. Since Maldon is an ancient town, we have centuries-old customs and traditions, but some are relatively new such as the Mad Maldon Mud Race. In December we have two Victorian Evenings that are par-

ticularly well attended which dates back as long as I can remember. The roads are closed to vehicles for the evening and the Christmas lights and decorations are already in full swing. All of the shopkeepers and traders dress in period Victorian clothing and there is a candle lit parade along the High Street. Susan particularly likes to attend this event. It is a well-attended function with thousands of people turning up from the surrounding villages. There are musicians and so on who participate and monies are collected to support the various charities we have here in Maldon.

The Panto

Traditionally, most families who could afford it always took their children to a pantomime or 'panto' as it is affectionately called, over the Christmas holidays. The rowdy response from the children to the cleverly crafted audience participation by the performers, always led to a wonderful afternoon of fun and laughter. Children would scream, 'He's behind you!' when a character in the play was creeping up on another individual on stage, followed by the retort from the performer, 'I can't hear you!' And so it went on, as the performers acted their way through yet another favourite story from our past.

Mike Edmonds, a Billericay man, has been performing in local and European Pantomimes for over ten years. His favourite character of late was his role as the Alderman in *Jack and the Beanstalk*, but there is

The panto. (Mike Edmonds)

no limit to his acting abilities. He has performed at Stratford-upon-Avon in the Royal Shakespeare Company's version of *The Lion, the Witch and the Wardrobe* and literally dozens of movies, pop videos, commercials and radio programmes.

In 1981, Mike appeared with *The Goodies* (Bill Oddie, Tim Brook-Taylor and Graeme Garden) as they perform a Christmas Special.

Mike recalls:

> For years, I was a DJ working with my Southend mates, doing discos, weddings, bar mitzvahs – all sorts of gigs before going into acting.

> Then, after my first acting part in the Ken Loach film, *Blackjack*, I was offered a part in *The Empire Strikes Back*. Since then I've become a regular on the *Star Wars* convention circuit in Japan, America and Europe where I sign autographs and meet many *Star Wars* and Trekkie fans. Other roles in movies such as *Return of the Jedi*, Terry Gilliam's *Time Bandits* and *Who Framed Roger Rabbit* have all been great roles for me. I've been lucky in being offered so many different parts.

Mike now lives in Southend-on-Sea but he grew up in Billericay and attended Billericay School in the late 1950s. Mike's parents acquired the shop at Hart's Corner in 1958 and then took over the Lake Meadows Café, also in Billericay, until they moved to Southend-on-Sea.

Greenwoods

Over the centuries, the uses of, and life at Greenwoods has changed many times. In 1947, after the current owner and squire of Stock, Adam Ellis died, the property was purchased by the West Ham Central Mission. A bold new programme for boys under the direction of Gladys and Bill Bodey was put into action. They sought the help of another couple, Megan and Fred Beagles, and together they provided the necessary support, training and guidance for the boys in their care.

In 1948, on a beautiful summer's day, the Queen Mother opened Greenwoods as The Country Centre of the Mission to a happy and joyful assembly. These were particularly difficult years in England. The stresses from the Second World War had left many families in dire need of emotional support especially for young boys who often fell in with the wrong crowd and found themselves in trouble with the law. For almost twenty years, Gladys and Bill Bodey ran a successful home until they retired in 1965.

After the retirement of Gladys and Bill Bodey, Reverend Ronald Messenger was asked to take charge of Greenwoods. It was a huge responsibility and undertaking, but was accepted gladly by Reverend Messenger. He remembers fondly the work he and others did at the Mission. In his book, *The Greenwoods Years* he gives a detailed account of those people instrumental in the success of Greenwoods as well as a personal look at Christmas time.

The following extract from *The Greenwoods Years* was given with kind permission of Reverend Ronald Messenger:

> Merging the preparation into the normal daily schedule was a gentle encouragement for everyone to be involved. Occupational therapy in the work unit produced goods for the pre-Christmas sales in the house and in the Standard Telephones Basildon factory. The outside group brought in fuel for the log fire and great branches of holly from the woods. In the house decorations prepared, brass and silver polished to provide a tangible atmosphere of warmth and welcome. When there were children in the house our veteran resident, Elsie Cooper, unpacking her costume box, turned them into angels and shepherds for a nativity scene in the chapel. Then there was the home-made pageant written by someone on a contemporary but seasonal

theme, while others practised their artistic and stagecraft skills. The scenery was undeniably original. The public audience filling the hall for the performance received this masterpiece with Christmas charity, whether in truth they were bemused, baffled or blessed. For several years the Folk Choir of Billericay Catholic Church filled the second half of the bill with a lively concert of carols.

In early December the conference room was turned over to Santa Claus and kept locked to preserve his secrets. Gifts came in from many directions, churches, schools, clubs, charities and individuals; games, dolls and teddy bears, clothes food and money. There were seventy-five or more big bags, each to be filled with six or seven gifts wrapped and labelled. Every guest was allocated to a member of staff to see that a special personal present was bought and included in the sack. Forty or more stockings had to be well packed for those sleeping in the house. By the grace of God the provision made through widespread generosity ensured that by Christmas morning no bag or stocking was empty.

The morning began early; the turkey had to receive its final dressing for the oven, and soon after 7 a.m. a small team moved along the landings serving tea in bed with the stockings left by Father Christmas on his first visit (he would return later) in the silent hours of the night. The soft toy looking out of the top of each stocking often had surprising effect, as though it touched the child in the adult, whatever the age.

At 10 a.m. the hall was overflowing; neighbours and friends from the village and beyond joining the community for the morning service. A hundred extra chairs squeezed into every space, the stairs were occupied to make a tiered gallery, and then it was standing room only. In front of the congregation, to the right of the log fire blazing on the wide hearth, was the nativity scene. Life-size models begged from

a Chelmsford department store now skilfully dressed as Mary and Joseph; straw from the farm covering the floor and making a bed for the child in the manger. A special touch of realism was given one year by the baby of one of our young mothers; when the children came forward around the manager to sing their favourite carol with 'No crying he makes', baby Roy happily co-operated.

Anne, our nurse at that time, describes the art of preparing one of the guests for the service. If Roy was the youngest member of the household that Christmas, Miss Davy was certainly the oldest. She was brought from her lonely East End flat each year to spend a week or two with us. At the last count, she was ninety-nine years old. Her great spirit and ability to enjoy the change of environment among such a crowd made her a much-loved guest.

Pealing bells broadcast to the village sounded the welcome as the setting gathered all ages, residents and visitors into the warmth of Christmas. Items in the service were sometimes unusual; once as the congregation sang, *I saw three ships* – they were surprised to see three ships 'sailing' down the aisle, beautifully crafted in the work unit.

Soon after midday order was restored, and the catering team, trying to remain cool and calm in the kitchen, were inspecting the turkey, counting the sausages, making the stuffing, heaving great pots of vegetables, unwrapping the puddings, and whatever else had to be done to feed seventy or more expectant Christmas diners. The dining tables were a picture of festivity, with the best white cloths decorated with flowers and candles and crackers at every place.

When visitors arrive at Greenwoods today they may be excused for not knowing the history of this magnificent building. For many years, Christmas parties have been held within its walls bringing happiness and caring at a time in an individual's life when it was so desperately needed.

Greenwoods. (Greenwoods Hotel and Spa)

Greenwoods is now a luxury spa and hotel but yet maintains all the beauty of those bygone years. Christmas is still enjoyed, but in different ways. Claire Knott, sales and marketing manager at Greenwoods said she appreciates the fine workmanship and beauty in the home. She stresses that management has tried to update yet maintain the integrity of this beautiful seventeenth-century building much of which remains unchanged to this day.

Claire Knott notes: the building retains much of the original workmanship. I particularly like the sweeping staircase in the original

building, the library area and the huge fireplace in the main lounge. The panelled windows are in keeping with the time period, as are the bedrooms and other function rooms. The spa was added five years ago and although this is relatively modern, the theme of the building has been maintained so it all blends nicely together.

I understand there were some pleasant gatherings at Greenwoods at Christmas time, and that the building has a long and interesting history. We continue that tradition by having some nice events too. We host a Christmas party and a New Year's Eve Gala event in our heated marquee in the beautiful landscaped gardens. A classical singer and pianist entertain our visitors in the Rosewood Restaurant whilst they enjoy a traditional lunch on Christmas Day.

We are very proud that we have been able to maintain the beauty of this old building whilst bringing it into the twenty-first century. Visitors can still enjoy the wonderful old surroundings and accommodation and yet take pleasure in the state-of-the-art luxury spa.

In Good Hands at Warley Barracks

Now ninety-seven years of age, Chelsea Pensioner, James Reddell of Brentwood recalls what Christmas was like for himself and his family at Warley Barracks from 1936 to 1939. The soldiers that were trained at the barracks were shipped throughout the world, but they knew their families were in good hands especially at Christmas time.

James Thorn's *Handbook to The Environs of London* dated 1876 described the Warley Barracks as:

> On the S. side of the Common are the extensive Warley Barracks. They were originally erected by the East Indian Company as a depot for recruits; purchased by the Government in 1842 for £17,000 for a depot for the Royal Artillery, and are now an establishment for the Infantry, with accommodation for 1500 men. To fit them for their present purpose they have been much altered and added to, the sanitary arrangements improved, and a roomy and handsome chapel, Byzantine in style, erected from the designs of Mr M.D. Wyatt.

Due to the unrest in various parts of the Empire, the government realised they needed a fully equipped, trained armed force of men that could be dispatched as and when needed. Camps were set up throughout England for this purpose and Warley Barracks had literally thousands of men pass through the doors for training and then sent around the world. King George III visited the barracks and

Above and right: In good hands at Warley Barracks. (James Reddell)

Dr Samuel Johnson inspected the camp, but he gave it an unfavourable report sighting the unhealthy conditions under which thousands of soldiers existed. The men lived in tents, were rigorously trained and discipline was particularly harsh. Reddell reminisces:

> Christmas was always a lively place over Christmas and the New Year because there used to be a huge party in the mess with plenty of good food and presents under an enormous Christmas tree. The atmosphere was lively even though many soldiers were serving overseas – everyone looked forward to the holidays as Christmas merged into the New Year. We always had a slap-up meal at the barracks and the officers would wait on the privates – so really the tables were completely turned around in a manner of speaking. There were obviously some sad times too especially during the war when our men and women were shipped off, but those who stayed behind always tried to make the best of things.
>
> Later, when the barracks were razed to the ground to make way for the Ford Motor Co., it was a sad time, but I try not to dwell on the old days too much – after all, life goes on.

Welcoming Prisoners of War

It is hard to believe that just after the Second World War there were more than 500,000 prisoners of war located throughout England. They were kept in 'camps' close to towns and villages and were required to help with the rebuilding of England especially repairing bridges, roads and railways. Away from their loved ones, these young German prisoners of war experienced the generosity of the people of Essex. David Sparks of Brentwood remembers when just such a soldier came for Christmas dinner:

> I remember the incident vividly because the back gate opened and in walked my mother with this (to me) huge man dressed in full German uniform. My dad was in the army and home on a forty-eight-hour 'kit up' and I wondered what his reaction would be but he just stood up and said 'hello soldier'. They shook hands and I remember our visitor clicked his heels together as a kind of formal salute. The conversation was limited because we spoke little German and our visitor's understanding of English was limited too, but we managed to understand each other with gestures and sign language. He told us his name was Hans Leman, and he asked the names of each member of our family. We had a wonderful dinner which, when I look back on it, must have been really difficult for my mother because everything was on ration. After dinner we showed Hans our family photograph albums and he took a real interest in everyone.

Welcoming prisoners of war. (David Sparks)

Hans asked lots of questions, he would hold up an item and ask us how to pronounce the word, he was interested in everything! We took him to our Glad Tidings Hall on the Queen's Road for a service later that day. He sang *Silent Night* in German and I remembered being fascinated that he actually knew the song – of course, he sang it in his own language.

Hans was very clever with his hands. He made my mother a needlework box and, when he saw my new Meccano set that I'd got for Christmas, he made me a fantastic wooden box to keep all my pieces in. He even painted it blue and yellow and put my name 'D.J. Sparks, Meccano Box' on the lid. I remember being thrilled with that box! He also made several different toys. One in particular was a monkey that did somersaults. These were simple but clever devices wherein Hans used two pieces of wire (I think he used coat hangers) then he placed the monkey between the wires and somehow made it spin backwards and forwards. Using the same technique, he made a clown too. Hans was a clever man.

Later, other prisoners of war came to our Glad Tidings Hall and we had them back to our house and made them welcome. I'm not sure how long we were friends with Hans and the other men, but I do remember it was long enough for me to get attached to Hans. He eventually went back to Germany and his family but he knew I would be upset when he took his leave. Instead, my mother said he came by our house early one morning while I was still asleep and left a book by my bedside that he had inscribed: 'You will have success and remember your friend.' We kept in touch for a while but like most things … our lives moved on as I'm sure Hans' life did too.

You know, when I think of what my parents did at that time – they were good, loving and forgiving people who believed they needed to set an example to their children – I think they did that for us.

David's wife, Anne, whose family also attended Glad Tidings Hall, recalls a particular Christmas as a little girl when she was given the fairy off the Christmas tree. Anne smiled at the sudden recollection, '… I remember the fairy was very pretty, and had a lovely dress made of blue net.'

Santa and Reindeer

Dennis Rookard, a lifelong resident of Brentwood finds himself particularly busy over the Christmas holidays as he and the staff of Eastwood Hospital Television prepare special programmes for a video magazine titled *Essex in Vision*. These programmes are circulated free of charge to over sixty local South East Essex hospitals, nursing homes and old folks homes, giving much pleasure to viewers.

Over the years, Dennis and company have produced all manner of Christmas programmes and entertainment including carol singing, dancing and other presentations. One year, the children from a local school were filmed as they sang Christmas carols in a farmyard setting complete with farmyard animals as props.

This past Christmas, Dennis went into the Essex countryside to capture on film the relatively new concept of decorating the outside of homes as well as the inside. Usually, just a lighted Christmas tree could be seen in the window of a home, but now people have become quite creative with the outside too. Santa can now be seen on the roof or in the process of climbing down a chimney – things have changed quite a lot since Dennis was a child, as he recalls:

> Like many other kids at the time, I never realised I was deprived in any way. My parents and I lived in a two-up and two-down cottage with gas for lighting and cooking, candles and oil lamps in the bedrooms and an outside toilet at the end of the garden – didn't everyone?

At Christmas, I was always so excited about the thought that Santa would be coming that I tried to stay awake to witness his arrival, but I never did and always went to sleep. Then I used to wake up before my parents on Christmas morning and race to the window to see if snow had fallen – it never did. But then my attention quickly went to the sack, or I should say pillow case, that was at the bottom of my bed because I could see there were things inside and I knew Santa had been. My sack was always full of toys, sweets and books. I always remember getting an *Eagle Annual* which was one of my favourite books. But one year, I got a portable radio – a special treat!

Since we didn't have electricity there was obviously no television but during the Christmas holiday we used to listen to a large battery-powered wireless. The radio was only used in the evening as we listened to *Dick Barton* or *Journey into Space* with everyone hoping the battery would last though these great programmes. When I wasn't listening to the radio, I was reading, as I've always had a voracious appetite for books.

Christmas dinner was always a chicken, never a turkey. I don't think my mother really enjoyed the taste of turkey to be honest, but we always had a bottle of rather nasty sweet wine at dinner and ginger wine that we bought in Romford.

As an adult I've had my fair share of fun at Christmas. I was even roped into being 'Santa' at a large store in Basildon. There I was sitting in my little grotto with an elf to assist me (usually a young girl taken from the cash register) as I fielded the questions from children. I followed my usual routine, ancient dusty book in hand and, when the child approached me I'd ask the question, 'Have you been a good boy/girl' answer to which was invariably, 'Yes'. Then on to the next question, 'Well, I can see that you upset your mum by not wanting

to go to bed early last month'. The child would always look down at their feet and not utter a word in the fear of jeopardising the visit. But mum would be smiling at this point and I'd slam the book closed and announce, 'Never mind, just so long as you don't upset your mum again. Now what do you want for Christmas?' This would open the flood gates, as both Santa and the child were now on the same level and were firm friends.

There was one little visitor to my grotto who was more than I could handle. The little chap did not believe that I was Santa because he'd seen Santa that morning in Southend, ten miles away, so how was it possible for him to be in two places at the same time. 'Very simple

Santa and reindeer. (Dennis Rookard)

I told him – a trick of the trade. You've heard of the time dilation theory?' Well of course he had – what young lad hadn't (or didn't want to admit that he hadn't) heard of the theory, 'Well, that's how it's done', I replied. That seemed to satisfy him because he asked no further questions, which was just as well because I hadn't a clue what to say next!

One last memory of my stint at being Santa was from a very young girl who approached the grotto with her mother and, after a little back and forth humour, I decided to ask the child what she thought her mother would like for Christmas. She looked me straight in the eyes and with a serious look she replied, 'A man!'

One of the most often asked questions during the many appearances and events over the Christmas holidays is, 'What is the name of the reindeer?' I think he goes by the name of Trevor during the year but he doubles as Blitzen at Christmas time.

Everyone at Eastward Hospital Television tries their best to make the Christmas holidays a pleasurable event – in fact; we're already planning Christmas 2007!

Party at the Nick

Peter Kent, who once lived in Brentwood and is the son of a police officer recalls times when his father was not available to have Christmas dinner with the family. It was something he and his brothers got used to because after all, crime did not stop for the holidays, in fact, it was often worse:

> My father had to be extra vigilant over the holidays because that was a time when stolen goods were being shifted from one place to another. There was always a great demand for cigarettes, household wares – just about anything! Farmers were scared that somebody would raid their farms and take the turkeys that had been fattened ready for Christmas. I remember that sometimes, dad had to spend the whole night watching and waiting for thieves and one night in particular, dad returned home in the morning with severe chaps on his legs because of the terrible cold. When I think back, it was a hard life for him especially as the nights in Essex can be merciless, but I never heard him complain.
>
> There were some good parts to being the son of a policeman as Peter remembers the wonderful Christmas parties: It was something to look forward to – there was always a nice tea complete with bloater-paste sandwiches, sausage rolls, mince pies and always a trifle, as seen in the photograph. We were served lemon-barley squash and sometimes even lemonade; everything was supplied by the parents. After our party, we played games such as pass the parcel and blind man's bluff

Right and below: Party at the nick. (Peter Kent)

until Father Christmas arrived (later identified as the inspector) and gave each of us a little gift. We all had a good time together, bearing in mind that several of our fathers were on shift work, so it was especially nice to be together.

A Community Christmas

The Christmas Tree Festival in Brightlingsea began as a relatively small affair but now comprises more than 100 entrants each year. Spokeswoman for the Christmas Tree Festival, Nola Bloor, said the festival provides a real community spirit at Christmas because the festival goes far beyond the display of the trees. Bloor commented:

> Our festival has non-stop music throughout the two days of celebration. The musicians are drawn from all age groups – children learning the piano can practice performing a Christmas carol, local musicians play jazz, the junior school choir perform and the university choir all participate in the event. There is also an organ recital and a brass quartet; in fact, all aspects of the community are represented and get a chance to perform in person.
>
> We also have a wonderful refreshment stall and amazing home cooked cakes all contributed by local people. The finale of the festival is a glorious carol singing evening in our packed church.
>
> All-in-all, we have more than 250 people who help, organise and promote the Christmas Tree Festival each year. It is truly a community

> experience that is great fun and of course provides a generous donation to local and national charitable causes. We anticipate 8 and 9 December 2007 to be as successful as our previous years … or even better!

The Festival began in 2003 with fifty-seven entries that raised £3,834 for charities. Since 2003, the festival has not only doubled in size, but it has also doubled in contributions with a staggering amount of £6,750 collected at the Christmas 2006 event.

The organisers of the festival have established four categories for entrants: Best Group Tree, Best Individual Tree, Best Children's Group Tree and Best Individual Child's Entry. Visitors to the festival vote for their favourite trees. There is a prize for the winner in each category.

In addition to individuals, all manner of organisations participate in the festival from nursery groups, schools, Brownies, Guides, police departments and retirement homes. Participants regularly bring a sense of fun to their entrants, such as the police group's tree was called 'Special Branch' the book group's tree was titled 'Litertree' and the children's version was 'Virtual Realitree' which comprised children's drawings of a Christmas tree set in a PowerPoint presentation.

The Brightlingsea Police Department decided to take the challenge in 2006 and enter the competition for the first time under the Best Group Tree category. PC Jo Bennett and station office assistant Linda Hyams went to work on the 'theme' of their tree. They used police colours of black and white with flashing blue lights accented with tiny replicas of high visibility yellow jackets – for that extra touch of colour.

PC Jo Bennett said, 'We have all had a tremendous amount of fun in thinking of ideas and making the themed tree. Christmas is a

demanding time for the emergency services, so to be able to participate in the tree festival was a pleasant distraction.'

Making the decorations was a family affair as station office assistant, Linda Hyams recruited the help of her daughter, Laura, and PC Jo Bennett enlisted the help of her two daughters, Mia and Emily. The group willingly spent their evenings making the decorations and was thrilled to hear the tree had won first prize. The win has only whetted PC Jo Bennett and Linda Hyams' appetite and they are already planning the tree for Christmas 2007.

The War Years

Christmas during the war years was particularly harsh for many families throughout England but particularly in Essex which was second only to London in taking the brunt of the German attacks. Dawn Hyde (nee Vincent) recalls that an uncle lost his life on the Thames which was a frequent target for the German air force. Dawn's own father worked as a tug captain on the Thames and he and his family knew his life was often in peril. Happily he survived, even though while living with his father in London, with his wife and twin daughters, the house sustained a direct hit. They all survived, but moved to Hullbridge soon after and loved living in Essex.

Dawn remembers the special Christmases they had in Essex even during the war:

The war years. (Dawn Hyde)

I know it must have been very difficult for my parents during the war – but I must admit that I never fully appreciated the danger we were in and how hard it must have been for mum and dad. When the sirens went off, we all used to run down to the shelter at the school which was only a matter of yards from our house. We used to cover our heads for protection and carry our gas masks as we ran. I remember that my gas mask had a picture of Mickey Mouse on the outside. Anyhow, we'd all run to the shelter with our dog running alongside us. Then we'd have to wait in the shelter until we heard the 'all clear' siren and then we'd come out and go about our normal day.

We moved to Hullbridge in about 1940, just after the war started. It was a lovely place to live, close to the water – everything was fresh and clean. There was only a three-room school with outside toilets across the playground that used to freeze up during really cold weather. My teacher, Miss Anderson (she may have been married, I don't recall) used to make a real effort every Christmas by decorating the class with wonderful pictures of Jesus, the nativity and other symbolic Christmas scenes. The whole feeling was one of happiness and security despite the bombings. Mostly, we were safe living in Hullbridge because London took the brunt of the bombings.

Since I am a twin, we girls always used to dress alike and mum used to have a seamstress in Hullbridge who would make identical clothes for us. It was a good time at Christmas because we always got a new outfit, some toys and lots and lots of sweets. This was because my uncle had a sweet shop in London close to Custom House, so he would bring bags and bags of sweets to us at Christmas time.

As I said, I have a twin sister who was born ten hours after me – in fact, that's how we got our names. Since I was born in the early morning, my parents named me Dawn, and my sister, Eve was born in the evening – hence the name of Eve. We loved Christmas! There was no television in those days of course so jigsaws, snakes and ladders and other board games were played over the holidays. As we were twin sisters, we slept in the same bed and one Christmas Eve, we were sure that 'Santa' had just come in to our bedroom and touched our feet. We screamed with excitement! Such happy times!

In 1945, our younger sister Carol Ann was born, so there were now three girls in the family. We often played with those cut-out dolls and dressed them in all sorts of fashions and designs. We always seemed to have a Christmas tree but I remember one year when we had a very

small tree that had to be dug out of the garden. Even though it was small, we still decorated it with real candles – little white candles that we lit on Christmas Eve.

I look back with such fond memories of my life as a child in Hullbridge especially at Christmas. It was a good life and one that I remember with great affection. Now my grandson, Jamie Spinks, has bought a house in the area, I am looking forward to spending many happy times with him and his family.

Sailing Club Tradition

In 1975, the Clacton-on-Sea Sailing Club began a wonderful tradition called the Frostbite Flask Race. Initially there was a trophy for the overall winners of a series of races held during the winter months and, since it was a winter activity, only those members who were known as 'diehard' or 'foolhardy' entered the contest. Although there is no actual record of how many people participated in the first race, the winner of the race trophy, a flask, was D. Heightman and Commodore Phil Stanton made the inaugural presentation.

Over the years, the event has changed little other than becoming a single race event held on Boxing Day. The winner still shares the contents of the flask with the other members of the race, but in 1986 the event was renamed The Hot Toddy Race. Winner of the 2005 race, press officer Dan Eagle recalls the history of the Hot Toddy Race:

Sailing club tradition.
(Clacton Sailing Club)

The season basically stops at around the end of October when our club has its Laying Up Supper. At that time of year, the Winter Series preparations begin with the checking the sea-worthiness of boats, including the rigging and making minor repairs, etc. Then comes the Hot Toddy Race which is open to all members of our club regardless of age or gender. The race usually appeals to the 'die hard' or one could say 'foolhardy' (I include myself in this) members of our club. There could be as few as three or as many as twelve or more club members participating in the race.

The race begins only after consideration has been given to weather conditions. The race generally consists of a triangular course beginning at the clubhouses outer distance marker (ODM) which lines up with the race box on the clubhouse's balcony to form a start line. All

participants leave at the same time although there is a handicap based on PY (Portsmouth Yardstick) calculations.

The winner of the race usually shares the contents of the flask with the other participants as a goodwill gesture. The winner's name is etched on the flask and that person is allowed to keep it for the full year until the next winner is designated.

The Hot Toddy Race is purely a pleasurable and amusing event meant to entertain our members and provide some winter fun. However, we do have a summer regatta that raises money for our local lifeboat charity.

Over the years, the race has been cancelled due to inclement weather. The safety of the participants has always been the primary concern of the club, so if there is any doubt, the race will be cancelled. After all, this is a family affair and so there is no need to place people in harm's way.

The Salvation Army

When General William Booth began his crusade to help the poor and destitute of London in 1891, he could not have imagined the impact he would have on the less fortunate of our society and indeed the world. Over 100 years have passed, but his principal plan to train men in a worthwhile profession so they could eventually support themselves and their families has grown immeasurably. Today, The

Salvation Army can be found worldwide helping people in need regardless of any religious affiliation or nationality. They bring hope and happiness, food and clothing, not only throughout the world but also in local communities.

Beverly Egan, The Salvation Army's Director of Social and Community Services in Essex provided the following:

> The Salvation Army traditionally provides a Christmas dinner during the Christmas period for at least 500 people in Essex. While most of the activity occurs on 25 December, some meals are provided on Boxing Day and the week before Christmas Day. These meals are given to individuals who would otherwise be on their own or would have difficulty cooking or obtaining a hot meal during the festive season. The Salvation Army centres provide meals free-of-charge or at a basic price. These meals are financed by donations, money made from street collections, or through sales at charity shops in the run-up to Christmas.
>
> The meals provided are turkey dinners complete with fresh vegetables and all the trimmings, supplied by supermarkets and businesses. They are prepared, cooked, served and cleared-up by volunteers who will also transport guests to and from Salvation Army centres. Some meals are delivered to shut-ins or the disabled and volunteers generally entertain the diners until the Queen's speech is broadcast at 3 p.m.
>
> Diners include clients at a Salvation Army resettlement centre for homeless people in Braintree, residents at an elderly care home in Southend, and people sharing meals at community churches in Essex on Christmas Day.
>
> The Salvation Army is a Christian church and registered charity that began in the East End of London in 1865 but which has expanded

The Salvation Army.
(The Salvation Army)

to 111 countries today. Remaining committed to its Christian principles, the basic aim is to meet human need without discrimination – and welcomes people of all faiths and no faiths, of all backgrounds to share meals and other support services.

Sharing the real meaning of Christmas in the local community and helping those less fortunate through practical Christian love is a pri-

ority for The Salvation Army at this time of year. So you'll often see Salvationists playing in a band on a street corner, in a shopping mall, or outside a hospital providing carols to passers-by; collecting toys to distribute to needy families and for social services; hosting community carol services both indoors and outdoors; or providing meals for people at community churches throughout the region.

It's a busy time for Salvation Army members and volunteers but caring for the homeless, the elderly, single parents, families on low incomes and the lonely and unloved are year-round activities.

This work couldn't happen without the support of Salvation Army church-goers and volunteers from the community – including people from other religions and those who profess no faith at all. The Salvation Army accepts almost any help that is offered, but asks that would-be Christmas volunteers get in contact as soon as possible so that they can be fully prepared and given training or reference-checked where necessary. Many volunteers return each Christmas to help out with the meals, while Salvation Army programmes need volunteers throughout the year to help with community and church programmes.

Besides volunteering, those in the community can support the Salvation Army by fund-raising for this work, donating to a Salvation Army centre or charity shop.

The Salvation Army's Farm

Life at the Salvation Army's farm in Hadleigh does not stop for Christmas or any other time of the year. The animals still have to be fed and tended regardless of outside activities. Simon Gibson manages the Salvation Army's farm, and his wife, Ginny, manages the Rare Breed Centre. Both have their hands full especially when they have to juggle their work schedule around the Christmas holidays and their family.

In 1890, William Booth, founder of the Salvation Army, published a book titled *In Darkest England and The Way Out*. In the book, Booth described his vision of helping the poor and destitute by providing them hands-on education in an agricultural environment or other life skilled job that could change their lives. Part of that plan was the farm at Hadleigh which has the distinction of being one of the first outreach programmes offered by the Salvation Army in Essex.

General William Booth purchased 800 acres of farmland around Hadleigh with the purpose of implementing his master plan. The purchase was not seen as a particularly sensible idea since the land was considered by the local people as 'badlands' and not suitable for farming. Nevertheless, Booth's plan went into action and he acquired another 200 acres of land making a total of more than 1,000 acres that were owned by the Salvation Army.

Since the inception of the programme and the death of General Booth in 1912, more than 7,000 men have been trained at the

Hadleigh farm. They were educated in a wide variety of farming techniques including livestock, poultry, market gardening and orchards. Their experience was not limited to farming, but also included pottery making and bricklaying. This was all part of General Booth's plan, to educate a man so that he could provide for himself and his family.

For the last few years, the Gibson's have enjoyed running the farm, each with their respective duties. Simon has one fulltime employee, Dave Wheeler, who has worked on the farm for sixteen years and Pete Howe, who, at seventy-three years of age, still enjoys working on the farm. Ginny manages the Rare Breed Centre with a little help from time-to-time from seasonal workers. The Christmas holidays do not create a problem for the Gibson's who take it all in their stride. They recall their last Christmas celebrations at the farm:

> Last year, we held three carol services in the barn. One was for the Hadleigh Training Centre located on our site and about 100 people attended – all trainees, their parents and staff. The second service was for the Thundersley Congregational church which was celebrating their 100-year anniversary. Ginny and I have attended the church for over four years, so it was especially nice to have a service in the barn and celebrate with our congregation. We managed to entertain more than 200 people with the help of the farm animals! The goats climbed on bales of straw piled 8-ft high – everyone seemed to enjoy the activity of the animals and this created a great atmosphere. The third event was on Christmas Eve and hosted by the farm and the Hadleigh Training Centre. We opened to the public who came by the hundreds to enjoy the service and to see the livestock. Ginny and I gave readings as did two members from the Hadleigh Training Centre. Heather, the

chaplain of the Hadleigh Training Centre also spoke to the attendees; it was a good day for everyone.

Life for us on Christmas Day is much the same as any other day – we begin as usual at 6.30 a.m. and feed the animals. Then we spend time with our children Josh, Joel and Naomi as we all open our presents and enjoy the morning, then we go to church. Later, after we've had our Christmas dinner, we go back to check on the animals – that's the last thing we do at night.

We plan on continuing our Christmas programme and even expanding it as years go on. The main thing is to remind people what Christmas is all about – that's our aim.

Granddad Playing Santa

Linda Arthey (nee Newton) recalls what Christmas was like in Dagenham after the Second World War. Most items at that time were either on ration or simply not available. If they were available, they were probably cost prohibitive for most ordinary families. All wished they could place a plump turkey on the table, but at best a capon or even a rabbit or two would have to do. Parents did what they could to provide a special feast for their families even during post-war London.

Linda always remembers a packed house at Christmas time. Her grandparents' house in London had been bombed so they, together

with their son Tom were taken in by Linda's parents. They shared the house as so many people did in those days; Uncle Tom had the 'box room' whilst Nan and Grandad had the rooms upstairs and downstairs at the back of the house. Linda and her parents shared the upstairs and downstairs in the front of the house:

> That's how people behaved in those days, no family member was ever turned away especially if they were bombed out – we simply made room for them. Having a relatively large family, made it nice at Christmas because there was always something going on, especially when aunts and uncles came over to visit. My aunt Eva liked to play the piano, so inevitably, there was a sing song. We used to have our traditions like most families. Dad and I would go by bus to Green Lane to get a large box of Quality Street sweets. I've wondered since if there was a shop that sold Quality Street closer to where we lived, but perhaps dad just liked the tradition of going to this particular shop every year. We also had the dreaded box of dates – nobody ever ate them, so I don't know why they were bought in the first place. I suspect it wasn't Christmas unless we had the box of dates sitting on the sideboard! There they sat – sometimes until Easter!
>
> My 'big' present was always a new coat and sometimes a pair of shoes, but it was the stocking at the end of my bed that gave me the most pleasure. Well, it wasn't a stocking as such, but a pillow case which I suppose was more practical. I always had sweets, apples and oranges, nuts and small toys in the 'stocking'. I don't recall seeing a banana for several years until after the war had finished because they were a real luxury.
>
> On Christmas morning, we used to open our presents and I'd usually play with my new things while mum started the dinner and she

Grandad playing Santa. (Linda Arthey)

and dad visited with other members of our family or neighbours. In the early days, mum and dad used to listen to the Queen's speech on the radio, but then we got a television set when I was about five years old, so things changed somewhat. Mum and dad, and anyone else who was visiting used to stand when we listened to the national anthem even if we were right in the middle of dinner! Mum's homemade Christmas pudding was served (whether you liked it or not) and after that the children who were present would get dressed up and do little 'plays' for the grown ups.

When I look back at those times, they were happy! We didn't have a lot of money but we looked after each other in times of need. I don't recall there ever being a lot of alcohol consumed – people just seemed to appreciate the people around them. Dad used to do 'his bit' by dressing up as Santa for the children's parties each year. I'm sure my son Damien wondered why on earth granddad was dressed in a red suit and wore a long white beard – but he didn't say a word!

An Essex Man

Captain Lawrence Edward Grace Oates had a distinguished career in the Inniskilling Dragoons and was known for his courage and stubbornness during battle. During one engagement he was wounded badly by a gunshot to the leg, but still he would not admit defeat. It was this incident that led to his nickname 'No Surrender Oates' but he eventually succumbed to the bitter weather of an expedition to the South Pole.

Oates had always been a headstrong young man growing up in the country home of Gestingthorpe Hall, Essex. When he reached manhood, he joined the Inniskilling Dragoons. He had a successful career in the military, proving himself of strong character and a good leader of men. He loved the sea and always imagined that one day he would own a boat of his own. He also loved to be around horses and showed an unusual skill and understanding of the animals that

perhaps led to his securing a coveted position on Scott's expedition to the South Pole.

When Capt. Oates realised that Capt. Scott was planning an expedition to the South Pole, he asked to join him. Scott was impressed with Oates' abilities and he gave him responsibility for caring for nineteen Manchurian ponies that would carry the expedition's supplies.

In June of 1910, the *Terra Nova* was fitted out and set sail. Five months later, after sailing to New Zealand, news came that Amundsen, the Norwegian explorer, was also mounting an expedition to the South Pole. A race was in progress as to which party would be the first to succeed and plant the flag of their respective country.

At first the expedition seemed to be on schedule but then, on Christmas Day, the ship became icebound. Nevertheless, the crew rallied and made merry. They had a wonderful meal with plenty to drink which put them in good spirits. Each member of the crew was encouraged to sing their favourite song, Oates chose 'The Fly is on the Turnip' which according to Miss Broadwood, who published English County Songs in 1893, was a favourite among soldiers.

Unfortunately, the expedition did not arrive at the South Pole before Amundsen's team. Scott and his men must have been devastated when they arrived at the Pole and saw the Norwegian flag planted firmly in the snow. Still, they celebrated their arrival with a meal, photographs and drinks. After planting the Union Jack next to the Norwegian flag, the group turned their attention to the journey back home which would prove fatal for them all.

The journey to the Pole had taken its toll on the horses and dogs which had either fallen into crevasses or had to be destroyed because of deteriorating health. Now the men slogged through the snow and

Left and opposite: An Essex man. (Donald Wallace)

ice as their feet became frost bitten and both their health and spirits dwindled.

Oates' feet were probably the worse frost-bitten of the group, but still Capt. Scott encouraged him to continue until a fateful day when Oates announced after a fitful night's sleep, 'I am going outside, and I may be some time.' He was never seen or heard from again. All members of the party knew that Oates was sacrificing himself for the benefit of the group, in the hope that without him as an impediment, they would return safely home. However, the group did not

return safely, instead they perished in the unforgiving climate. Capt. Lawrence Oates' selfless act was only discovered much later when Capt. Scott's diary was found with the bodies of himself and the other men. Scott wrote: '…we knew it was the act of a brave man and an English gentleman.'

When Capt. Oates' mother learned of her son's death, she mourned for him and moved into his bedroom that had been left unchanged since his departure. On 8 November 1913, a plaque was erected in the church at Gestingthorpe, it reads:

In Memory of a very gallant gentleman Lawrence Edward Grace Oates. Captain in the Inniskilling Dragoons born March 17 1880 died March 17 1912 on the return journey from the South Pole of the Scott Antarctic Expedition. When all were beset by hardship he being gravely injured went out into the blizzard to die in the hope that by so doing he might enable his comrades to reach safety. This tablet is placed here in affectionate remembrance by his brother officers AD 1913.

Masquerade Ball

As one of the largest and most prestigious inns in Chelmsford for centuries, the Saracen's Head Hotel has hosted many Christmas parties and balls including the Flowerists Feast and the Chelmsford Beefsteak Club. These clubs, together with many others held their annual parties at the inn during the eighteenth century, but last year, on New Year's Eve 2006, the inn hosted its first Masquerade Ball. It was such a huge success, plans are already in the making for the ball of 2007.

For almost 500 years, Chelmsford has been known for its excellent inns both in town and the immediate vicinity. A famous map by John Walker prepared in 1591 mentions the Saracen's Meade (or garden) and in 1622, Daniel DeFoe notes that Chelmsford was 'full of good inns'. In 1724, Thomas Nicholls, a property developer raised £600 to build the inn, but he over extended himself financially and defaulted

Masquerade ball. (Donald Wallace)

on the loan. In 1738, Nicholls lost the property and it reverted to his creditor's nephew and heir, William Taylor.

Now, centuries later, the residents of Chelmsford still recognise the inn as an important place in the community where meetings, weddings, parties and all kinds of special events are held. It is also a favourite place for visitors, especially those who enjoy the history of the hotel.

General manager of the Saracen's Head Hotel, Rachael Tappenden, recalls the lead up to the Masquerade Ball of 2006:

> Since this was our first year of hosting the ball, I was unsure as to how it would be received in the community – I did not need to be concerned because we sold over 600 tickets! The highlight for me was when the doors opened and I could see the amount of time and effort the participants had taken on their costumes. Some of the masks were very impressive, and ranged from scary to classic, although some people wore vintage masks as well. It amazed me to see the extraordinary lengths our guests went to and the amount of fun the evening generated. We will certainly entertain other Masquerade Balls in future years.

A Family Affair

As a child, Roger Pickett of Aveley had no intention of becoming a fireman. It was not until he was in his early twenties that his future father-in-law, Ron Turrell, suggested he do something other than driving a lorry for a living and 'do something worthwhile'. Ron Turrell had been in the fire service himself since 1947, and felt it was a meaningful occupation and one that he thoroughly enjoyed. Early in the summer of 1976, Roger applied for a job in the fire department, was put through the tests, and interviewed by 'menacing' senior officers. He passed the tests and so began his career as a fireman.

Fighting fires runs in the family. Roger, his father-in-law Ron Turrell, his brother-in-law, Trevor Turrell, and also Roger's son, Leigh have all joined the fire brigade. Leigh Pickett has worked for the Essex County Fire and Rescue Service for over ten years remembers:

> I never anticipated becoming a fireman when I was a child. My life was like that of most other children during the 1950s growing up in Essex and was filled with family, school and friends. I lived with my parents, brother and sister in Grays and recall a very happy childhood especially at Christmas which was always a special time. When I look back, I wonder if I showed my appreciation for all that my parents did for me … I don't suppose so, when you're a kid you just kind of accept things.
>
> Dad worked in the oil industry and by comparison to other families in the area, he was well paid and could afford some nice things for us at Christmas. We always had a stocking at the end of our beds on Christmas morning, and I remember the excitement when I stuffed my hand in the stocking to get the things out. There were always some nuts, a banana and one of the smaller presents (that could probably fit in the stocking), and a tangerine! To me, a tangerine was something that was 'exotic' – I can still smell those tangerines to this day – they always bring such pleasant memories of Christmas time.
>
> I don't remember ever seeing mum or dad collect the stocking, fill it up or put the stocking at the end of my bed. As far as I was concerned, it was a magical thing – oh, the innocence of it all.
>
> When I was a child, I used to play in a sand pit next to the Grays Fire Station. I'd watch the men from the station doing their drills, running up and down ladders and doing other manoeuvres. When they

A family affair. (Roger Pickett)

saw children in the sand pit, they would squirt water over us which caused much laughter. I remember being impressed by the men's uniforms and the big red fire engines – it seemed like an exciting life to a young, impressionable boy. Never in my wildest dreams did I ever think I would become a fireman myself!

In 1973, I married Gill and we've now celebrated 34 years together. We have two children, Cheryl and Leigh. Leigh has continued the tradition of fire-fighters in our family. Leigh understands the commitment to the fire brigade even through the Christmas holidays. After all, he grew up without having his dad at the Christmas dinner table every year. The job of fire fighting is like no other with hours

of waiting … but then, we have to be ready to leave the station in seconds. Christmas is no different from any other time of the year and indeed some fires are started with candles left unattended. Sometimes, children (and adults) do not realise the dangers of a naked flame and how quickly the situation can get out of hand.

We usually have about thirteen firemen on duty over the holidays, but this varies from county to county and indeed over the country. It all depends on the number of fire engines at the location. Christmas dinner is of the traditional variety with turkey and Christmas pudding. We always have far too much food prepared, but we can let off steam by having a food fight. The excess food becomes the ammo and the target is usually the watch officers. They take it all in good spirits, and then there is a good clean up afterwards. No harm done and besides, it's good for morale.

I have recently retired from the fire department and have realised my dream of opening the very first Firemen's Museum in Grays. I will be the part-time curator of the museum which is scheduled to be opened in June, 2007. There will be many artefacts and exhibits. In particular, my own three fire engines: a 1953 Dennis F12 pump escape, a 1954 Dennis F8 pump and a 1968 Dennis F38 pump. All engines are in roadworthy condition and full working order. There will also be many photographs because, as a keen amateur photographer, I always carried a camera when I went out on call. I have taken some good photographs such as the one on Christmas watch – note the hats!

All in all, my life in the Essex County Fire and Rescue Department has been a worthwhile profession and, even though at times it has been dangerous and upsetting, for me it was the best job in the world!

The Great Essex Hunt

Hunting in Essex is an age-old tradition that has withstood controversy, foot-and-mouth episodes and saboteurs, but none has stopped the event which is still enjoyed, especially during the Christmas holidays. The Essex Farmers' and Union Hunt meet on Christmas Eve, Boxing Day, New Year's Eve and New Year's Day. Secretary, Sarah Henderson commented on the hunt:

> The Christmas Eve meet is traditionally aimed at the younger members of the field (the collective name given to those who follow the hunt), Santa often makes an appearance, horses are dressed in tinsel and there is a great atmosphere of anticipation prior to Christmas Day. This is usually a short hunting day, as the grooms have to get the horses cleaned and settled, and also clean all the tack and clothing ready for Boxing Day.
>
> Christmas Day begins with presents, of course, but there are then horses to muck out – they all get presents too!! The anticipation builds up once again for Boxing Day, the high point of the hunting calendar. It really is a case of best clothing, top hats come out of their boxes for one day only, best pink coats and immaculately turned out horses are necessary for the showcase event. Many hunts meet in local high streets or on village greens across the country. The general public is more than welcome to attend any hunt meet, but Boxing Day has a real traditional place in the lives of some. People arrive, wearing their

The great Essex hunt. (Private collection)

new clothes, wrapped up against the cold with their children, grandchildren, all to see the spectacle of the hunt moving off. The hounds are incredibly friendly, and they love children and having a fuss made of them, so Boxing Day is great for them! The horses that carry us behind the hounds all have a wonderful temperament – a good hunter is worth his weight in gold. They are all calm beyond belief, dearly loved and cherished. They adore the attention too, and to see a small child's face light up when he is held up on the back of a proud hunter is the best sight in the world. The Boxing Day meet makes Christmas for so many people, including the riders. To move off for a day's hunt-

ing, feel the horse grow underneath you and to hear the cheers and whoops of support is really a fantastic feeling.

After Boxing Day, the next major day is New Year's Day, which again usually involves a meet in the local town. The Essex Farmers' and Union meet in Maldon, Essex. The High Street setting again creates a marvellous atmosphere, the horses' hooves echo off the overhanging buildings, as do the cheers of supporters.

Mumming Plays

The ancient tradition of mumming plays can be traced to Greece when strolling players called at private houses to perform a short play, either depicting a mythical tale or a story of love or wooing. Their visit was believed to bring good luck and fertility to the home and surrounding area, so the visit was much appreciated by the homeowner. Recompense for the visit was often given in the form of food and wine.

The centuries-old tradition of mumming plays at Christmas time is still alive and well in Essex. There are variations in characters, dialogue and costumes depending on the play and the location, but the time-honoured theme of goodness prevailing over wickedness is always the same. The hero/combat plays involving St George fighting and killing the Turkish Knight who is then 'cured' by the doctor (or shamanic) is probably one of the favourite plays in Essex.

Over the years, the group known as the 'Fabulous' Thameside Mummers has collected more than thirty different plays from around the country. The group is in constant demand and performs locally and nationally. Traditionally, they have no need for props since they constantly move about and therefore the scenery on route becomes the backdrop to the play. They wear theatrical costumes to represent the part of a particular actor, St George for instance would wear a white tunic with a red cross and the jester would wear a suitable costume complete with bells! The plays are still performed around the time of the Christian festivals such as Christmas and Easter which is sometimes known as 'Pace Egging Time'.

Richard Peacock and Derek Oliver both members of the 'Fabulous' Thameside Mummers describe how the group collects stories and maintains the tradition of mumming plays:

> Plays have been discovered from villages all over England, mostly collected by local gentry or churchmen and written in their diaries or books of 'local customs'. The tradition even reached Wales where the Mari Llwyd (Grey Mare) and her entourage would visit homes and perform a ritual song/play in return for food.
>
> The villagers would perform their play but once each year, the parts being handed down from father to son; the costumes would be a suit of rags, with each character being introduced by the wording of the play, 'In come I … ' or by a 'calling-on' song. These rags would be simple and cheap to produce but would also hide the 'real' identity of the performer, important if the play included some line, or ad-lib, critical of the church or the local gentry. For this reason, the mummers would frequently blacken their faces with soot to hide their identity.

Mumming plays. (Fabulous Thameside Mummers)

As with the ancient Greeks, the performances of the play would be associated with gifts from the audience, normally in the form of food and drink. The mummers would of course perform for the lord of the manor and his guests, expecting (and probably receiving) a considerable amount of food from the kitchen and wine from the cellar. Nowadays, the remuneration tends to be in the form of cash, though a free pint or two and the occasional meals are gratefully received and faithfully consumed.

Few village plays are still performed in their original locations, but many have survived to this day and are kept alive by some teams of

Morris dancers who include one or two plays amongst their dances and by a few teams of mummers who perform many different plays both at the traditional celebrations and through the year at festivals and fairs.

Frost and Snow

The following extract was published in *An Essex Christmas.* The author Humphrey Phelps has kindly given permission for its use in this book.

1814 January, temperature below 27 °F.

1837 20 January, temperature -4 °F. Players wore skates to play cricket on frozen Gosfield Lakes.

1841 January, deep snow at Colchester.

1854 4 January, heavy snowfall, deep snow at Colchester. Railway services between Colchester and Norwich suspended.

1860 Mid December, skating on Wanstead Pond. Christmas Day Temperatures 8 °F.

1881 18 January, blizzard lasting twenty-four hours. House and trains buried in snow, lifeboats capsized, barges sunk, parts of South Pier swept away. Snowdrifts of up to seventeen feet.

1890 13 December, skating on River Can at Chelmsford.

1891 Early January, over two thousand skating on river between

Chelmsford and Maldon.

1893 Early January, Ice Carnival on The Cutting.

1894 5 January, temperature at Chelmsford 0°F.

1895 February, very severe frosts cause great hardships.

1906 White Christmas Day. Roads blocked. Heaviest snowfall for fifteen years at Clacton.

1917 Long cold winter.

1918 January, heavy snow.

1927 White Christmas. Roads blocked. Finchingfield, Bardfield, Dunmow, Halstead isolated for a week.

1928 January, snow.

1938 White Christmas. Snow every day in Essex from mid-December.

1939 Snow at end of December.

1940 January, snow, severe frost. Heavy snowstorm for three days middle of month.

1941 Cold winter with snow.

1942 January, snow fell at Romford on seventeen days; and on nineteen days in February.

1945 January, very cold, snow on ground half the month.

1947 20 January, very severe weather started; and continued for two months. Temperatures down to -5 °F. Some rivers frozen. Snowdrifts of fifteen feet.

1950 Coldest December since 1890. Snow at Romford for eighteen days.

1951 1 January, heavy snowfall.

1962 Coldest Christmas since 1897. Snow fell on Boxing Day, most of Essex under snow until March 1963. 1962-3 coldest winter since 1740.

1968 Snow in January. Some rivers frozen.
1969 February, snow on ground at Earls Colne for a fortnight.
1970 White Christmas. Heavy snowfalls on Christmas Day and Boxing Day.
1978 Snow at end of December.
1979 Snow in January.
1980 Snow in December.
1981 Coldest December since 1890, with snow at Colchester for three weeks.
1982 January snow.
1985 January, temperature fell to -12 °C at Colchester for a fortnight.

The following data is included with the kind permission of George Booth from Epping.

1986 Snow in January and December.
1987 Severe frost and heavy snow in January. Thin covering of snow mid-December.
1988 Snow in January.
1990 Snow in December.
1992 Snow in December.
1993 Snow in January and December.
1994 Snow in January.
1995 Snow in January and December.
1996 Snow in January and December.
1997 Snow in January and December.
1998 Snow in January and December.
1999 Snow in January and December.

2000 Snow in December.
2001 Snow in January and December.
2002 Snow in December.
2003 Heavy snow late January with further snow in December.
2004 Snow in January.
2005 Snow in January and December.
2006 Snow in January
2007 Snow in January.

White Christmases

George Booth does not remember too many white Christmases in Essex as a child or even as an adult. He does believe his interest in weather conditions began as he and his family travelled back and forth to Scotland and North-East England, where his extended family lived. He noticed how the weather patterns changed during the long journey. It was a fascination that developed over the years into a lifelong hobby of tracking weather conditions and collecting weather records. Now retired, Booth reminisces on his childhood and his interests:

> My childhood Christmases were spent in a small village in County Durham in the North East of England. Since my father was an engineer, I tended to get presents of a practical nature in the form of Meccano and Hornby Dublo kits. Each Christmas I would get the

White Christmases. (George Booth)

next box up in the construction kit or model railways series. When I was in my teens we moved south to the London area.

With family links in the northeast of England and Scotland we certainly did a lot travelling in those years, especially over the Christmas holidays. The travelling probably prompted an interest in weather patterns because we went through many contrasting areas. I began keeping weather records in the 1960s, but it was not until 1979 that I kept these on a more formal basis. When I retired in 2001, I decided to organise the records and add them to my weather website. In 1983, I started flying gliders and have continued flying to this day. It is a great activity with plenty of fresh air and the opportunity to experience the weather close-up.

Customs and Traditions

The Tree

We owe the Christmas tradition of bringing a tree into the home to decorate to Queen Victoria and Prince Albert who noticed the practice during a trip to his family in Germany. The royal couple liked the concept so much, they adopted the idea, and so began the custom of Christmas trees in England. The regal tree was lit at night with lighted candles which were carefully watched by the staff.

At first, only the more affluent homes in Essex had Christmas trees inside their homes but later the tradition spread to the other classes, and even those who could not afford such a luxury would at least have some kind of evergreen foliage such as mistletoe, holly or ivy to decorate their homes.

Since few people owned a car in the early 1940s or 1950s, the man of the house usually had to hand-carry the tree from a greengrocers shop. The trees were usually around 4ft high and would be tied around with string keeping the branches secure. The greengrocer would make a handle out of string so that it could be easily carried. Once home and set in a pot of soil, the string holding the branches would be cut, allowing the branches to spring out. Sometimes, families would wait until Christmas Eve to purchase their tree in the hopes of getting a bargain at the grocer's shop.

Greeting Cards

We can thank Henry Cole for the invention of the Christmas card. In November of 1843, Cole, who was then assistant keeper at the Public Record Office, was so busy that he knew he would be unable to hand write his Christmas letters, so he devised a unique way to solve his problem. He commissioned John Calcott Horsley, an artist, to design an image, place it on a card with space for a simple message and another space for the addressee. Horsley created a scene depicting the poor being fed and clothed and an affluent family enjoying Christmas. This was accomplished on a lithograph measuring 5½ ins x 3½ ins. One thousand of the hand-printed, hand-tinted cards were produced. Henry Cole took as many of the cards as he needed, and the balance was sold on the open market for 1s each.

Soon the tradition of sending Christmas cards spread to Essex as entrepreneurs saw the opportunity for a growing business. During Victorian times, the cards became more stylish with layers of lacy paper, glitters and other embellishments and were sold in the better-known shops such as William Wilson in Brentwood.

Kissing Boughs

One of the most popular customs at Christmas is the act of kissing under the mistletoe. Sometimes, there would be just a simple sprig hanging over the doorway but other times the foliage would be made into a kissing bough. The origin of this particular tradition is unknown, but mistletoe was thought to be a sacred by the Druids who sought it out around the winter solstice and used it in their pagan rituals. It could be found growing as a parasite on oak trees in the forests of England, its waxy leaves and berries during winter months must have seemed mystical to the ancients.

Charles Dickens describes the use of mistletoe at Christmas in *Pickwick Papers*:

> From the centre of the ceiling of this kitchen, old Wardle had just suspended with his own hands a huge branch of mistletoe, and this same branch of mistletoe instantaneously gave rise to a scene of general and most delightful struggling and confusion; in the midst of which, Mr. Pickwick, with a gallantry that would have done honour to a descendant of Lady Tollimglower herself, took the old lady by the hand, led her beneath the mystic branch, and saluted her in all courtesy and decorum.

Yule Log

The burning of the Yule log appears to be a pagan ritual found throughout the world. Robert Herrick (1591-1674), born in Cheapside and described by A.C. Swinburne as, 'the greatest song-writer ever born of English race' wrote a poem describing the Yule log tradition and the necessity to light the log with the remnants of the previous year's log. In the poem, he stresses the importance of having clean hands to ensure the fire will burn well:

Come, bring with a noise,
My merry, merry boys,
The Christmas Log to the firing;
While my good Dame, she
Bids ye all be free;
And drink to your heart's desiring.

With the last year's brand
Light the new block, and
For good success in his spending,
On your Psaltries play,
That sweet luck may
Come while the log is a-tinding.

Another poem for the young women:

Yule log. (Victoria Wallace)

Wash your hands, or else the fire
Will not tind to your desire;
Unwashed hands, ye maidens, know,
Dead the fire, though ye blow.

Whenever possible the root of an ash or oak tree would be used for the log. It was hoped the log would last for the twelve days of Christmas. Any remnants would be kept to use as kindling for the following year. By retaining and using the kindling each year, there was a belief the fire never ceased but continued from one year to the next.

Crackers

The Christmas cracker originated from an idea by Mr Thomas Smith. In 1847, he returned to England from France where confectioners were wrapping sugared almonds in twists of waxed paper. Smith took that concept a step further by wrapping his sweets and placing them in attractive boxes. He was constantly aware of the competition and therefore always looking for something different. It was not long before he invented the tube-like container that was wrapped in brightly coloured crepe paper, added the paper hat, motto, small trinket and the fun of pulling the cracker to get the 'crack'.

Dorothy Whisker of Dagenham recalls when she first saw Christmas crackers appear on the table:

> Mum and dad used to buy two boxes of crackers, one large and one small and 'put them away for Christmas'. The smaller crackers used to be put on the Christmas tree as decoration. I don't think they had anything inside – just the crack when they were pulled. The larger crackers were always kept for Christmas dinner and were put by the side of our plates. We used to pull them before eating our dinner because we wanted to wear the paper hat, enjoy the small trinket inside and read those mottos. I remember how silly those mottos used to be – they were really awful sometimes. And there were some years when we didn't get crackers – I believe that was either during or after World War II but they were important to us – the silly mottos made us laugh – they were part of Christmas.

The Robin

One of the most delightful birds seen at Christmas time and probably the most featured on Christmas cards is the robin redbreast. Robins are so closely associated with Christmas time that many myths and legends surround the friendly little bird.

One the most popular tales is that a little brown robin tried to remove the thorns in Jesus' crown and, as he did so, a droplet of His blood fell on the robin's breast turning it red in the process.

Another tale is that a robin who tried to fan the dying embers in the stable where Christ was born. In doing so, one of the hot embers fell out and turned the little bird's breast red, but he continued regardless with his duties in an effort to keep Jesus warm in the manger.

Yet another story concerns a superstition that if one sees a robin first thing on Christmas morning, one will have good luck in the coming year. Needless to say, many people provide all sorts of incentives to get the little bird to visit their homes. They provide crumbs, tiny pieces of meat and suet to encourage the little feathered friend to gather where he can easily been seen. A favourite rhyme:

Robins and wrens
Be God Almighty's friends.

The Wren

On Boxing Day, there used to be a cruel and merciless tradition that thankfully is now no longer practiced; it was called the 'Hunting the Cutty Wren'. It involved young boys going into the woods to capture a wren for their own pleasure and amusement. Sometimes the wren would be caged for the whole twelve days of Christmas, paraded around town as they offered a glimpse of the bird for a special treat. At the end of the twelve days, the wren would be set free. At other times, the wrens were not so lucky. Their poor lifeless bodies would be pinned to a bier as the naughty boys chanted a song. There are many variations of songs or chants. Following is an example:

Wren. (Victoria Wallace)

The wren, the wren, the King of all birds,
On St Stephen's day was caught in the furze,
Though he be little his honour is great,
Therefore Good People, give us a treat.

Boy Bishops

An ancient custom believed to have originated in the thirteenth century involves the selection of a boy from the local church to become a 'boy bishop' for three weeks beginning 6 December, Saint Nicholas' feast day, and ending on 28 December, Holy Innocents' Day.

The boy, once chosen by his peers, would be addressed as St Nicholas, Bishop of Myra and patron saint of children. He would enter the church wearing a smaller but identical version of the Bishop's robes complete with mitre and crosier and take his position on the throne. He would be attended by other boys who assisted him during his three weeks of service. The boy bishop was expected to conduct most of the ceremonies normally carried out by the acting Bishop, with the exception of giving Mass. On his final day, as 'bishop' the boy was expected to address the congregation and preach a sermon. He was also required to lead a procession through his parish blessing all those who came out to watch the spectacle.

Originally, boy bishops were appointed only in cathedral cities, but later the custom spread to smaller parishes throughout England.

During the nineteenth century, this delightful ritual was once again revived in East Anglia by the Reverend H.K. Hudson in the village of Berden, located close to Saffron Walden, Essex. The practice continued each December and was enjoyed by the parishioners until 1937, when Reverend Hudson left the village.

The tradition has not always been popular. King Henry VIII suppressed the concept in 1541 because he felt it was 'unfitting and inconvenient'. But when Henry's daughter Mary I came to power in 1554, she revived the custom perhaps believing it was good for the church. When Elizabeth I took the throne in 1558, she abolished the practice again. However, over the past few years, there has been a resurgence of interest in the boy bishop concept, especially in some church schools in Essex.

Boy bishops. (Evelyn Gladstone)

A 'Thomasing' or a 'Gooding'

The 21 December is known as St Thomas's Day. It is the shortest day of the year and can also lay claim to a custom rarely practiced today. It was the custom for the poor ladies of a village to go house-to-house seeking charitable contributions to help provide their families with a decent meal at Christmas. This was obviously a form or begging, but one that seemed to be accepted in most villages and towns in Essex. The women could usually expect a 'donation' of approximately 6d.

Other terms for the custom are: 'going gooding' or 'goin' a-gooding'. In some parts of England, it was customary for the ladies to take a two-handled pot around to the more fortunate families in the village. This was called 'going a-corning' because the contribution would not necessarily be money, but a measurement of wheat (better known as corn). A song that may have been sung by the women:

Well a day, well a day,
St. Thomas goes too soon away,
Then your gooding we do pray
For a good time will not stay.
St. Thomas gray, St. Thomas gray,
The longest night and shortest day
Please to remember St. Thomas's Day.

The Holy Bible refers to 'Doubting' Thomas because he doubted Christ's resurrection and wanted proof:

John 20:24-29

Thomas (who was called the Twin), one of the twelve, was not with the other disciples when Jesus came. So the other disciples told him, 'We have seen the Lord.' But he said to them, 'Unless I see the mark of the nails in his hands, and put my finger in the mark of the nails and my hand in his side, I will not believe.'

A week later his disciples were again in the house and Thomas was with them. Although the doors were shut, Jesus came and stood among them and said, 'Peace be with you.' Then he said to Thomas, 'Put your finger here and see my hands. Reach out your hand and put it in my side. Do not doubt but believe.' Thomas answered him, 'My Lord and my God!' Jesus said to him, 'Have you believed because you have seen me? Blessed are those who have not seen and yet have come to believe.'

First Footing

During the period 1880-1930, the farmers of Essex suffered terribly from an agricultural depression. The cause of this depression was a combination of devastated harvests, an abundance of inferior wheat from abroad and a consequential drop in wheat prices. Unable to survive these catastrophes, the farmers had to sell their farms and move on to other ways of making a living.

The Scots took advantage of the slump in Essex and more than 300 Scottish families made their way south by train from Inverness. They brought with them not only their prized cows and expert farming techniques, but also their parsimonious habits. During the long and arduous journey to Essex, the farmers milked the cows which not only relieved them from their burden, but also provided sustenance for the farmers and their families on route.

The influx of Scottish families to the area meant they also brought with them their customs and traditions of Christmas and the New Year. One such custom is that of 'first footing'. Traditionally, a man with dark hair should enter the front door of the home at the stroke of midnight. He should not wear any dark clothes as if in mourning, he should not carry anything sharp, have bad thoughts and should not have a limp or be otherwise impaired. Depending on the area, he should carry specific gifts such as a piece of coal, or other means of providing warmth such as wood or peat; a bottle of whiskey, beer or mead, a loaf of bread or a cake and some silver coins. These gifts

First footing. (Victoria Wallace)

are symbolic of the need for warmth, food and drink and wealth. The dark haired visitor may also hold some kind of greenery – the universal sign of a messenger.

The visitor would enter in silence but after doing so would kiss all the ladies and recite a rhyme. Following is a Colchester version:

I wish you a happy New Year
A pocketful of money, a cellar full of beer,
A good fat pig to last all year
So please give a gift for New Year

After following this ritual, the visitor must exit through the back door to complete the custom.

Snapdragons

At Christmas time the Victorians loved to play games especially Snapdragon, a game that required dexterity and speed if one was not to get burned. It was usually played after dinner on Christmas Eve. The lights were extinguished and a large serving dish containing raisins or nuts was soaked in brandy or rum and set alight. The 'players' had to grab as many nuts or raisins as they could as they sang:

Here he comes with flaming bowl
Don't he mean to take his toll
Snip! Snap! Dragon.

Oranges and Lemons

A favourite game played in many Essex homes was the parlour game known as Oranges and Lemons. Two people were chosen from the party to be the leading players. They would secretly decide who would be an orange and who would be a lemon. The two individuals would clasp hands and hold them above their heads to form an

Oranges and lemons.
(Victoria Wallace)

archway. The other participating members would then file under the arch as everyone would sing:

Oranges and lemons said the bells of St. Clemons
I owe you five farthings said the bells of St. Martin
When will you pay me said the bells of Old Bailey
When I get rich said the bells of Shoreditch
When will that be said the bells of Stepney
I do not know said the big bells of Bow
Here comes the chopper to chop off your head!
Chip, Chop, Chip Chop – the last man's dead!

The person caught under the arch was quietly asked a question: Did they want an orange or a lemon? Once they made their choice, that

individual had to stand behind the respective person. The song would continue until each person had been caught by the 'chopper' made by the two leading players. The finale was a tug-of-war between the orange and lemon teams.

Terry Parson's was a lifetime resident of Brentwood. Unfortunately, he passed away a couple of years ago, but before that sad event, he recalled his childhood at Christmas and those wonderful games they used to play before television was invented:

> I used to love Christmas-time. I was one of a family of ten children living in Albert Street, Warley. There wasn't much money about in those days, but we all received presents in our Christmas stockings – we were happy with what we got. I can remember sitting down to Christmas dinner with the whole family. Because turkeys were more for the well-off, my mother would cook a cockerel and a piece of silverside and then, after dinner, we would sit around the wireless to listen to the King's Christmas message which was addressed to the country and the Empire. And of course, as there was no television as there is today, we played games and made our own entertainment.

Terry also remembered how the shops in the High Street used to decorate their front windows at Christmas.

> I can't remember the High Street being decorated, but every shop made some kind of effort to make really colourful window displays. Some of the larger family businesses such as Bon Marche and Wilson and even some of the smaller shops like Wildish, Lovells and Morgans really went to town with their decorations. It was a good to see each year.

Pass the Parcel

One of the all time favourites at children's Christmas parties was the game of 'pass the parcel'. The children would all be asked to sit cross-legged style in a circle and wait patiently for the music to begin. This usually came from a wireless radio, but sometimes from a gramophone. Then an adult would start the music and another would hand a relatively large parcel to a child in the circle and asked for the children to pass the parcel until the music stopped. When the music stopped, the child holding the parcel could remove one sheet of paper in the hope that he or she would get a little trinket or sweetie. Others were not as lucky as the parcel continued around the circle until the music stopped again and another child removed one piece of paper. This method of circulating the parcel with each child having 'a turn' until the whole package was completely unwrapped revealing the innermost present, was probably one of the most popular games played at parties.

Roasting Chestnuts

The smell of chestnuts roasting in the fire has always been one of those familiar, wonderful aromas that we associate with Christmas. In 1851, Henry Mayhew describes in his book *Mayhew's London* how vendors sold their wares in braziers to Londoners who enjoyed this seasonal delicacy:

> Then the tumult of the thousand different cries of the dealers, all shouting at the top of their voices, at one and the same time … 'Chestnuts all 'ot, a penny a score' … One man stands with his red-edged mats hanging over his back and chest, like a herald's coat; and the girl with her baskets of walnuts lifts her brown-stained fingers to her mouth, as she screams, 'Fine warnuts! Sixteen a penny, fine war-r-nuts.

As Londoners migrated over the border to Essex, they brought with them the tradition of roasting chestnuts in their new homes, always careful to make a small slit to avoid the chestnuts exploding in the fireplace. Even though many people purchased the chestnuts from the greengrocery, many people took advantage of sweet chestnuts that grew naturally in the ancient Thorndon Woods at Brentwood.

Linda Weiss who originally lived in East Ham and then moved to Harold Wood recalls times when she and her family collected chestnuts and roasted them in the open fireplace in a chestnut roasting

pan. She also remembers having hot cocoa drinks with a marshmallow on the top – a special treat:

> I always looked forward to Christmas because my mum used to take me to London every year to see the lights and we usually took in a show, or a pantomime. After that, we always went to C&A to buy a new coat. I got one every year, regular as clockwork. My current coat would become the one that I used every day for school, and my new coat became my 'best coat' used on Sundays and at other special times. So I suppose my Christmas present was really a new piece of clothing because I don't recall ever getting any big toys. Of course, 'Santa' used to fill our stockings each year with some nuts, a little inexpensive toy, a comic and an orange – nothing very exciting by today's standards, except that it was special to me.
>
> We really used to look forward to Christmas, decorating the house with all sorts of things – we had a Christmas tree but also dressed the house with a lot of those paper concertina type of decorations, Father Christmases, snowmen, and so on and then they could be closed down and brought out again the following year. We also made paper decorations out of those strips of coloured paper. Nothing was wasted, in fact, my cousin still saves her Christmas cards from the previous year and cuts them up to make gift tags for the following Christmas.
>
> If we were lucky enough to have some snow, we'd go sledding over at South Weald Park using metal trays or some form of plastic. We always amused ourselves and had fun. I think those days gave me a good foundation and values that I hope I've have been able to pass on to my own family.

Wishbone Tradition

The pulling of the wishbone, the V-shaped bone at the beginning of the breast area in a capon or turkey, did not take place at the Christmas dinner table because the bone was still too soft and pliable to break. Therefore, the wishbone would often be placed in the kitchen, usually on the window sill until it had completely dried out. Most people seem to recall that the tradition of 'pulling the wishbone' was done around the New Year. There always seemed to be arguments as to where each person was allowed to hold their part of the wishbone. The closer the top, the more likely that individual would get the biggest part and be able to make a wish. In some parts of England, the bone was called a 'merry thought' – the concept being similar except the person holding the smaller section is granted the wish.

A Friend at Christmas

The Benfleet home of Mr and Mrs Christopher Friend is particularly busy during the Christmas holidays. At Christmas time they gather together with other Pearly Kings and Queens of London and Essex at the church of St Martin in the Fields in London to attend the Pearly Court. The couple represent the Isle of Dogs in Poplar, but Benfleet is their home.

Although the Friends are in their late seventies, they are still very active as Pearly King and Queen raising money for charitable organisations as they have for over forty years. The events include opening bazaars, attending Little Haven Hospices and children's charities in and around Essex.

Mr and Mrs Friend have three children, nine grandchildren and many, many great-grandchildren.

The Pearly custom began in 1875 when Henry Croft, a young lad of thirteen years, left his orphanage to seek work in London as a rat catcher, road sweeper or worse yet, a mud lark, scavenging the Thames at low tide for anything of value. Croft was accepted by the costermongers and appeared to enjoy the company of these men who were known to 'take care of their own.' He liked the way they helped each other in sickness and how they assisted each other when they felt the police had been unjust. It is said that 'costers' never steal from each other and that one will watch another's stall while it is unattended without question or concern for loss of merchandise.

A friend at Christmas. (Mr and Mrs Christopher Friend)

The young Croft liked the way the costermongers dressed. On regular work days, they dressed in appropriate clothing for their trade, for instance a leather apron for a fishmonger, but on Sunday the costermongers would take a stroll with their ladies dressed in their finery. Croft noticed the decorative way some costers sewed a row of mother of pearl buttons along the outside seam of their trousers. He liked that idea so much; he began collecting mother of pearl buttons from the 'sweat shops' around the market and began sewing them on his clothes making intricate designs.

Over the years, Croft raised more than £5,000 for charity appearing in his Pearly King character. In 1930, when he died, more than 400 Pearlies followed in the funeral procession that was filmed by *Pathe News*. Nowadays, Croft's descendants carry on the tradition and keep this valuable custom alive, especially at Christmas.

A Storyteller

Jan Williams was born in Borth, Wales, and grew up hearing wonderful stories and intriguing mysteries such as those told of a sunken city below the waves, mystical forests and other legendary stories. It is not surprising therefore that after a lifetime of teaching history, English and drama that Jan would find something that encompassed all three – she became a professional storyteller. The career move came after she heard a storyteller, Taffy Thomas, perform at Sidmouth Folk Festival. She was so inspired by his performance that she decided to enter the 1990 Sidmouth Storyteller of the Year herself – and she won!

After moving to her home in Brightlingsea, Jan decided to further the concept of storytelling and formed a group called the Essex Storytellers; the purpose of the group being to meet other like-minded individuals, share ideas and information, and propagate the idea of storytelling. In time, the members became friends and began working together telling stories of Essex's history, oral traditions and

A storyteller. (Jan Williams)

even customs and traditions from around the world. The stories are often romantic and dramatic in nature and appeal to a wide audience. Sometimes the stories are performed at historical buildings such as Layer Marney Tower, but the venue varies and includes country parks, churches, museums and festivals.

Christmas is one of Jan's favourite times of the year to tell stories. She recalls being approached by Sheila Carrington, of Layer Marney Towers with an idea for a Christmas programme:

Most of the time I work on my own for more intimate tellings. A few years ago the organiser at Layer Marney Towers, Sheila Carrington rang me to invite me to tell at Layer Marney Towers, an historical location. 'We'll keep it simple' she said. 'I'll put a nativity scene in the barn with real farm animals, we'll floodlight the gardens, have a Father Christmas, and there will be mince pies, mulled wine and juice and you will tell stories'. It was intended to be a small scale affair but from the beginning there have been large crowds of children and parents eager to recapture the magic of a traditional Christmas, and lately I have noticed many senior citizens creeping in too to enjoy a good tale. It is such a joy for families to get away from the hurly burly of shopping.

The stories I tell there are fairy stories from all around the world and the different ways that places celebrate Christmas like the babushka in Russia and the Befana in Italy. *Cinderella* is very popular and the children are always fascinated to learn that there is a version of *Cinderella* which was told by a maid servant in Ipswich. The children love to join in and like repetition and rhyme and even the chance to sing. I have a special shiny jacket with a red velvet hat I wear for that Christmas telling.

I usually dress up to suit the occasion. Sadly I do not get as many Christmas bookings as I would like. I am busiest at Halloween because it is ghost stories which have such an appeal. My witch's hat is well worn and it has become the fashion to tell stories in the woods lit only by candles in pumpkins. I tend to give my ghost stories a twist of humour.

In the summer I tell at many outdoor events and have started to use a tipi as a lovely setting for storytelling and this means a lot of native American stories. I use hand puppets and book illustrations to help

A storyteller. (Jan Williams)

explain stories. Lately a black and white rabbit has become my most faithful companion. Animal stories are always popular.

I do a lot of storytelling to adult groups who enjoy tales with a local history connection, Celtic stories and tales with strong women characters. The stories I tell best and which I enjoy are linked to a landscape I know well for example the Welsh story of why seagulls cry is linked to my home village. Every telling is different even when I tell a story many times because the audience reacts differently, but I am always eager to find new material.

Plough Monday and the Molly Dancers

The event called Plough Monday is usually held on the first Monday after Twelfth Night. Richard Peacock of Southend participates in Molly dancing which is associated with the tradition of celebrating Plough Monday. Molly dancing is an ancient tradition perhaps of Anglo-Saxon origin and thought to be unique to East Anglia.

Richard's group (called 'side') is believed to be the only side currently performing traditional Molly dancing.

During the Second World War, the tradition of Molly dancing almost died out, but then, during the early 1980s there came a revival. Richard Peacock belongs to a side called Good Easter Molly (from the village of Good Easter). They perform each Plough Monday in various villages around Essex.

Richard Peacock notes the Molly dancers appear at schools to entertain and instruct the children so they learn the traditions of bygone years:

> My side is called Good Easter Molly and, as far as I know, we're the only side still performing the dances as near to when they were last recorded, without adaptation. We are not the only side in Essex, but we are the only side that perform the dances exclusively and during the proper season.
>
> We always try to appear at a school if possible to teach the children old customs and traditions. For instance, the period over Christmas was a particularly hard time for ploughmen since there was little for them to do in the fields, hence a lack of money. Traditionally, the ploughmen would try to get a few pennies by entertaining the village

Opposite: Plough Monday and the Molly Dancers. (Richard Peacock and Good Easter Mollys)

Right: Plough Monday and the Molly Dancers. (Sylvia Kent)

> folk. They did this by wearing their normal agricultural clothes, but they also blackened their faces as a disguise. The 'team' includes players acting the parts of the Lord and Lady of the parish. These two people are dressed in fine clothes so as to differentiate them from the main team. As the group moves through the village or town, money is collected and spent in the local pubs. Sometimes, the revellers get quite boisterous and rowdy, but as we have our faces blackened, it's hard for people to know who we are – after all, we're in disguise!

Another part of the tradition of Plough Monday was to place a corn dolly in the first furrow to be ploughed. The ploughmen believed that the corn goddess lived in the corn; therefore a corn dolly was made from the stalks of the previous year's harvest, placed in the

first furrow. By performing this duty, they believed her spirit would rekindle the earth and ensure a good harvest.

In north Essex, the plough used in the ceremony was painted white and kept in the local church until it was needed. For this reason the plough was known as the White Plough. As the time approached for the ceremony, the boys from the farm would collect the plough and decorate it with ribbons and bows. It would then be paraded around the village by the farm boys as they collected money from the farm owners and other gentry, then the money would be spent in the village alehouse. It was always wise to add a penny or two to their coffers rather than returning home to a front garden that had been completely ploughed!

Poets' Corner

Anthony Trollope at Waltham House

Anthony Trollope (1815-1882), the famous novelist wrote an autobiography that was published in 1883, a year after his death. In it, he describes his life at Waltham Cross, 'I settled myself at a residence about twelve miles from London, in Hertfordshire, but on the borders of both Essex and Middlesex, which was some-what too grandly called Waltham House.' After considerable improvements to the home, adding rooms and updating it, he settled down to the last years of his life. He particularly like the location as he was within easy reach of London but he also liked the grounds that surrounded the home, 'We had a domain there sufficient for three cows, and for the making of our own butter and hay.'

The happiness and personal achievements Anthony Trollope found at the end of his life was in stark contrast to his youth. He had a miserable childhood partly due to his family's background and social standing in society. His father, Thomas Anthony Trollope, had been a bright, intelligent barrister but his volatile temper caused him to fail at the bar. His efforts at farming were not successful, and then an expected inheritance from an uncle did not materialise. These events led to financial hardship for the family and in 1834, the family's monetary situation has worsened so much that Thomas Trollope sought refuge in Belgium to escape debtors' prison. In time, the whole family joined him, but it was his wife, Frances, who supported the family with her literary income.

Anthony Trollope. (Donald Wallace)

Young Anthony was not a happy child at school. His lack of status with his peers meant he was bullied and ostracised so much that he contemplated taking his own life at the tender age of twelve years. This sad episode in his young life seems to coincide with his mother's departure to America taking with her his three younger siblings. In 1831, after four years in America, and a failed business venture, Frances Trollope returned to England and quickly established herself as a writer.

Growing up, Anthony had been described as a daydreamer. Perhaps daydreaming had helped him through some of the more difficult times in his life. As an adult, he worked as a teacher but then took a position at the Post Office. He quickly gained prestige within that organisation and in 1841, was sent to Ireland where he met and married Rose Heseltine. A happy family life and his new position as Post Office inspector seem to have agreed with Anthony. He is credited by the postal service for the invention of the pillar box. Over the years, more than 156 designs of the pillar box were manufactured, often displaying the initials of the reigning monarch. In 1840, the Penny Black made its debut. It was the first stamp to have an image of a monarch, Queen Victoria, and also the first stamp to have an adhesive.

In 1867, Trollope left the Post Office to give his full attention to writing and was soon earning a reasonable income sufficient for his family's needs. Soon after his return to England from Ireland, he took residence at Waltham Cross and there produced some of his best works. In 1855, his first of six novels, sometimes referred to as *The Chronicles of Barsetshire* were particularly successful and these were followed by the *Palliser* novels. He was a prolific writer with a keen sense of humour and wit. His self-deprecatory humour and intelligence were appreciated by his contemporaries such as Thackeray and Eliot.

Charles Dickens

Although there is no absolute proof that Charles Dickens ventured deeply into Essex, there is strong circumstantial evidence placing him at various sites throughout the county. In his weekly journal titled *Londoners Over the Border*, Issue No. 390, 12 September 1857 he describes Canning Town and Hallsville marshes:

Charles Dickens.
(Dickens Fellowship)

> London does not end at the limits assigned to it by those acts of parliament which take thought for the health of Londoners. More suburbs shoot up, while official ink is drying. Really, there is no limit to London; but the law must needs assign bounds; and, by the law, there is one suburb on the border of the Essex marshes which is quite cut off from the comforts of the Metropolitan Buildings Act; – in fact, it lies just without its boundaries, and therefore is chosen as a place of refuge for offensive trade establishments turned out of town, – those of oil-boilers, gut-spinners, varnish-makers, printers' ink-makers and the like.

There are various other locations in Essex believed to be tied to Dickens. In James Thorn's *Handbook to The Environs of London* 1876, Thorn describes Chigwell and Dickens' association with the area:

> Chigwell Row consists chiefly of a line of good suburban residences on the N. side of the road, with one or two mansions, as Forest House (B. Cotton, Esq.); some cottages, and a couple of inns, the Maypole (commemorated in 'Barnaby Rudge' though this is not the house there described), and the Bald Hind, much frequented by Londoners in the summer season, though far less than before Hainault was disafforested and enclosed (1858).

It is rumoured that Dickens once visited the Lobster Smack on Canvey Island and that it was the inspiration of the sluice house mentioned in *Great Expectations*. Again, there is no absolute proof one way or the other that Dickens visited the area although he appears to describe the location particularly well. Following is an extract from *Great Expectations*:

Our plan was this. The tide, beginning to run down at nine, and being with us until three, we intended still to creep on after it had turned, and row against it until dark. We should then be well in those long reaches below Gravesend, between Kent and Essex, where the river is broad and solitary, where the waterside inhabitants are very few, and where long public houses are scattered here and there, of which we might chose one for a resting place. There, we meant to lie, all night.

Leaving the rest in the boat, I stepped ashore, and found the light to be in the window of a public-house. It was a dirty place enough, and I dare say not unknown to smuggling adventurers; but there was good fire in the kitchen, and there were eggs and bacon to eat, and various liquors to drink. Also, there were two double-bedded rooms – 'such as they were,' the landlord said.

Other places that Dickens was known to have visited are West Ham and Lime House in the East End of London. He frequented a pub in the East End called The Grapes. It was in this area when, as a boy, he was sent to work in a blacking factory and was known by the other factory workers as *The Little Gentleman*. The experience is said to have affected him for the rest of his life.

An extract from *A Christmas Carol*: ' … and it was always said of him, that he knew how to keep Christmas well, if any man alive possessed the knowledge. May that be truly said of us, and all of us! And so, as Tiny Tim observed God Bless Us, Every One!'

John Clare

Although he had limited formal education, John Clare (1793-1864) was to become one of England's most famous poets. His poetry often reflects the dialect of his Northamptonshire home, as well as county colloquialisms.

As a young boy of seven or eight years of age, he left school to work on a farm tending geese and sheep. A few years later, he got a job on another farm and went to school in the evenings where it is believed he learned algebra and therefore furthered his education as best he could. However, with his limited formal education he never fully adopted the standardised grammar seen in many of his contemporaries.

As an adult, Clare appears to have often been in poor health, perhaps due in part to poor nutrition as a child. He was short in height, barely 5ft tall, with a slim build and he was prone to sickness throughout his life. He tried successfully to support himself and provide for his parents with jobs that included the military, farm work and gardening. But, it was not until he purchased a copy of Thomson's *Seasons* and began writing poetry that his life changed. In 1820, his first book *Poems Descriptive of Rural Life and Scenery* was a great success. This was quickly followed by *Village Minstrel and Other Poems* that brought him much needed financial relief and recognition of his work, but it was not to last.

Clare married a local girl, Patty Turner, but the marriage does not appear to have had a calming influence on him. Instead, he was

known to visit the local tavern regularly and, in his own words, described himself as having a 'taste for ale.' As interest in his work declined, he found himself without a sponsor and therefore facing financial ruin. He tried to procure other venues for his work but he was unsuccessful and instead returned to the fields to earn a living. His fondness for drink and his delicate mental condition worsened over the years until he was finally institutionalised.

From 1837-1841, Clare resided in High Beach Asylum close to Epping Forest. He continued to write and some believe wrote some of his best work during this period. He had a remarkable talent for observing the countryside and animals, all of which he incorporated into his work using his Northamptonshire dialect and resisting the use of formal grammar.

Following is a short extract from one of Clare's poems.

Christmass

Christmas is come and every hearth
Makes room to give him welcome now
Een want will dry its tears in mirth
And crown him wi' a holly bough
Tho tramping 'neath a winters sky
O'er snow track paths and rhymey stiles
The huswife sets her spinning bye
An bids him welcome wi' her smiles
Each house is swept the day before
And windows stuck wi' evergreens
The snow is beesomd from the door
And comfort crowns the cottage scenes

Gilt holly wi' its thorny pricks
And yew and box wi' berrys small
These deck the unusd candlesticks
And pictures hanging by the wall.

By John Clare

Lord Alfred Tennyson

Lord Alfred Tennyson (1809-1892) was born on 6 August 1809, of George Clayton Tennyson and Elizabeth Tennyson. He was one of five children, two brothers, Frederick and Charles and two sisters, Mary and Emily. Emily had been engaged to Alfred's closest friend, Arthur Hallam a young man of twenty-two years whom he had met at Trinity College, Cambridge. Unfortunately, while Hallam and his father were in Vienna, the young man suffered a brain haemorrhage and died. When the news of Hallam's death reached England, Albert himself broke the news to Emily. By all accounts, both were emotionally devastated by Arthur's death but Emily found the strength to continue her life whereas Alfred was so distraught he even considered suicide.

After the death of Hallam in 1833, family and friends were concerned for Alfred's emotional wellbeing because he was plunged into a depression that lasted for months. In 1837, the family moved to Beech Hill House, High Beach, and here it seems that Alfred wrote

Lord Alfred Tennyson. (Donald Wallace)

much of his famous works *In Memoriam* in honour of his friend. One wonders if Alfred was inspired by the quietness and beauty of Epping Forest as he composed *In Memoriam* for his dear friend. *In Memoriam* is comprised of 130 poems. Following is a short extract:

In Memoriam

XXVIII

The time draws near the birth of Christ:
The moon is hid; the night is still;
The Christmas bells from hill to hill
Answer each other in the mist.

Four voices of four hamlets round,
From far and near, on mead and moor,
Swell out and fail, as if a door
Were shut between me and the sound:

Each voice four changes on the wind,
That now dilate, and now decrease,
Peace and goodwill, goodwill and peace,
Peace and goodwill, to all mankind.

This year I slept and woke with pain,
I almost wish'd no more to wake,
And that my hold on life would break
Before I heard those bells again:

But they my troubled spirit rule,
For they controll'd me when a boy;
They bring me sorrow touch'd with joy,
The merry merry bells of Yule.

By Lord Alfred Tennyson

Albert Tennyson became Poet Laureate in 1850 and remained so until his death in 1892. It appears that his friend was never far from his thoughts – indeed he named his first son after his dear friend.

Sarah Flower Adams

Born on 22 February 1805 in Harlow, Sarah Flower was literally a woman before her time. She married William Brydges Adams in 1834 when she was twenty-nine years old, but it was hardly a conventional marriage. She appears to have held unusual and unorthodox views on a woman's role in the household and, on agreeing to marry Adams, requested that she would provide 'no housekeeping' duties during their marriage. She was an early feminist who had unusual views and opinions about the roles of women during the early nineteenth century.

Sarah attended a Unitarian church in London then under the direction of the Reverend William Johnson Fox. She was a prolific writer who met many of her contemporaries such as William Wordsworth, Charles Dickens, Richard Hengist Horne and Harriet Martineau. While at the Unitarian church she helped Reverend Fox by contributing thirteen hymns and anthems to the publication *Hymns and Anthems* that was published in 1841.

Sarah was particularly fond of her elder sister Eliza, a talented musician. The two sisters were extremely close throughout their lives, but neither was to enjoy longevity. Both had long spells of ill health with one sister nursing the other through sickness. In 1846, Sarah succumbed to her illness despite Eliza's nursing. Perhaps the extra strain of caring and loosing her beloved sister was too much for her to bear, but Eliza too became seriously ill and died within two years of her sister's death.

Two of her most popular hymns are *He Sendeth Showers* and *Nearer, my God, to Thee.'* It is reputed that *Nearer, my God, to Thee* was played by the orchestra on the Titanic during the last hours. Following is a short extract:

He Sendeth Showers

He sendeth sun, he sendeth shower,
Alike they're needful for the flower:
And joys and tears alike are sent
To give the soul fit nourishment.
As comes to me or cloud or sun,
Father! thy will, not mine, be done!

Can loving children e'er reprove
With murmurs whom they trust and love?
Creator! I would ever be
A trusting, loving child to thee:
As comes to me or cloud or sun,
Father! thy will, not mine, be done!

Oh, ne'er will I at life repine:
Enough that thou hast made it mine.
When falls the shadow cold of death
I yet will sing, with parting breath,
As comes to me or shade or sun,
Father! thy will, not mine, be done!

By Sarah Flower Adams

Thomas Tusser

Thomas Tusser was born in Rivenhall, the fourth son of Isabella and William Tusser. There is some discrepancy as to the actual birth date of Thomas Tusser, some believing he was born between 1515 and 1524. But records show that in 1543, he was elected to King's College at Cambridge and since they would not admit any students under the age of nineteen years, that would place Tusser born in 1524. As a young boy he was a chorister, as an adult, a musician, poet and later a reasonably successful farmer. In any event, he was a restless character who moved around the country perhaps seeking his true vocation.

In 1553, Tusser married and settled down in Cattawade, Suffolk, on the Essex border. Here he seems to have been reasonably happy although his wife's health was a constant problem and she eventually died. He married again to Amy Moon and the couple was blessed with three sons.

Over the years, Tusser seems to have matured into a gentleman farmer but never seemed to attain the wealth that many of his counterparts enjoyed. He was responsible for the introduction of barley to his fellow farmers, a crop that did well in the arable soil of Essex. In 1557, he published his *Hundreth Good Pointes of Husbandrie.* In 1570, he expanded the volume to include *A Hundredth Good Points Huswifery* and then he continued to enlarge and expand on the publication over the next decades.

Tusser was a true lover of Christmas and filled his house with family and friends to celebrate the holidays. He would always encourage his friends and neighbours to give generously to the less fortunate during the holidays. Following is a poem by Tomas Tusser.

Christmas Cheer

Good husband and huswife, now chiefly be glad,
Things handsome to have, as they ought to be had.
They both do provide, against Christmas do come,
To welcome their neighbors, good cheer to have some.
Good bread and good drink, a good fire in the hall,
Brawn, pudding, and souse, and good mustard withal.

Beef, mutton, and pork, and good pies of the best,
Pig, veal, goose, and capon, and turkey well drest,
Cheese, apples and nuts, and good carols to hear,
As then in the country is counted good cheer.

What cost to good husband, is any of this?
Good household provision only it is;
Of other the like, I do leave out a many,
That costeth the husband never a penny.

By Thomas Tusser

Throughout his life, Tusser was an avid writer and eventually became an excellent farmer although he did not benefit much financially from his endeavours. Some say he died in poverty in May, 1580.

Thomas Tusser. (Elizabeth Wallace)

Later, Thomas Fuller said of Tusser, 'He traded at large in oxen, sheep, dairies, grain of all kinds, to no profit … and spread his bread with all sorts of butter, yet none would stick thereon.' Perhaps Tusser was aware of his misgivings because he liked to quote the expression, 'A fool and his money are soon parted.'

William Winstanley

Life for William Winstanley and others in the village of Quendon, Essex, were particularly harsh in the mid-1600s. The Puritan Parliament had issued a proclamation that '… no Observation shall be had of the Five and twentieth day of December, commonly called Christmas Day; nor any Solemnity used or exercised in the Churches upon that Day in respect thereof.'

Even as Oliver Cromwell tried to impose the statute of Parliament on the people of Quendon by locking the parish church on Christmas Day, the people rebelled. Instead they took the celebrations into their respective homes. Young men were sent into the woods to collect armfuls of winter evergreens such as ivy, holly and mistletoe that were used to beautify their homes. Families, friends and neighbours came together to sit around the fire, tell stories, eat, drink and enjoy games.

The celebrations began on Christmas Eve, with the house decorated and wonderful aromas drifting from the kitchen. Winstanley lived in a farmhouse called Berries that was located close to Quendon Woods. It was in the hall of the farmhouse that Winstanley entertained his family and guests as they sat around the fire smoking, cracking nuts and drinking wine. He would often quote a riddle, one in particular that obviously refers to the robin redbreast:

I am called by the name of Man,
Yet am as little as a Mouse.

When Winter comes I love to be
With my Red Target near the house.

Born in 1628, Winstanley was an ardent Royalist all his life. He believed Christmas should be enjoyed to the utmost. The celebrations at Berries began on Christmas Eve soon after the house had been decorated with evergreens and the food and wine began to flow. In true festive spirit, Winstanley and his family would play games and recite poetry.

Winstanley wrote Almanacs under the pen name of 'Poor Robin' (1662) the first of which was considered so shocking and outrageous that thousands of copies were sold.

The following extract is from a booklet by William Winstanley. The booklet is the property of the Saffron Walden Museum which has kindly given permission for its use. The booklet is titled *Poor Robins Hue and Cry*:

Poor Robins
Hue and Cry
AFTER
GOOD HOUSE-KEEPING
OR
A DIALOGUE
BETWIXT
Good House-Keeping, Christmas,
and Pride

... and every year when Christmas came to town invite three or four hundred of his neighbours to dinner, where they should not only feed but feast, and not feast but banquet:

Where Pig, Goose, Turkey, Capon, Cunney,
What might be bad for his Money,
Plum-Pudding and Furmity,
Mutton-Pasties Christmas-Pye,
Nappy-Ale, a full Carrouse
To the Master of the House:
Syder, Perry, and Strong Beer
For to wash down their good Cheer.

Local Poets

Ted Rogers, a Billericay resident was a late bloomer in his love of writing verse. He was eighty-three years old when his first poetry was published by 'Poets Corner' in Billericay Life, the monthly journal distributed until 2000 by the *Evening Echo* Series. Ted was inundated with requests from readers who loved to read his work, so he produced an anthology of fifty of his favourite poems and published them in a book entitled *Reflections*.

He is pleased his book has done so well especially as the funds from sales are distributed to local charities:

The Nativity

Christmas is here to awaken our thoughts
Of memories held dear

The fun; the laughter; old stories retold
We toast absent friends
Any pray for those left out in the cold
Further memories there's sure to be
Time to remember the meaning of Christmas
A babe born in a manger – the Nativity.

By Ted Rogers

Billericay

From the Rising Sun to the Crown
Rests the High Street of Billericay Town
A corner of Essex of great renown
The historic church centuries old
Wonderful stories it could unfold
Pilgrim Fathers in 1620 they tell
In the Chantry rooms tis said did dwell
To set sail in the Mayflower they planned
To cross the Atlantic to North American land
The ole Town Hall once busy and bright
Where local committees met night by night
The Cater Museum there you can see
Billericay life as it used to be
The readings rooms there at a tale
Of enjoyable events and bargain sale
The Red Lion with its decorative sign
Inviting you in town wine and dine
Older residents proudly claim

Past shop keepers knew each by name
May these few lines happily show
Nostalgic memories of long ago.

By Ted Rogers

God's Blessing

Christmas is for living, caring and sharing
To have a family we are blessed;
To keep your own loved ones God knows best
But life is for living and watching families grow;
So please God may we be together for eternity.

By Margaret Powell

Christmas is Here Again

Christmas time is here again, with snow upon the lawn,
My thoughts drift back to my Essex home, to the house where I was born.
Our humble home was simple, our needs and hopes were small;
Saving up for presents was the aim for one and all.
We climbed the stairs on Christmas Eve, singing our yuletide song
And hung our stockings on our beds, hoping Santa won't be long.
What happy times we had back then, no worries and no fears
Just carols round the fireside, no need for any tears.

We never had computers nor toys that cost a lot,
Our parents worked hard all year round for all the things we got.
The excitement of the Christmas tree, festooned with sweets and light;
Five sisters dancing round it, laughing with delight.
We 'girls' are so much older now, with children of our own
But we still remember Christmas in our happy childhood home.

By Evelyn Gladstone

Festive Fare

New Potatoes

During and after the Second World War, life in Essex was particularly hard, especially during the holidays when parents wanted to do something special for their families. Jack Bartlett of Billericay came up with an innovative and practical solution. Some time before Christmas, he filled old buckets with good quality soil and planted seedling potatoes. These potatoes were harvested just in time for the holidays, therefore giving his family an out-of-season treat.

Wartime Mincemeat

Stork is a registered trade mark of Unilever and the use of this recipe is with Unilever's kind permission.

Stork margarine made its debut on the tables of England in 1920 and coined the advertising slogan 'The Energy Giver.' In 1939, the Stork company offered recipes to housewives to encourage them to use margarine instead of butter. During that same year, when the Second World War broke out margarine did indeed replace butter on the table and, through necessity was used in cooking recipes.

Stork Wartime Mincemeat

1 lb raisins – stoned and chopped
1 lb sultanas cleaned
1 lb currents cleaned
½ lb Stork margarine (melted)
1 lb of apples, peeled and grated
1 lb candied peel, chopped
2 nutmegs, grated
½ lb Demerara or granulated sugar
Rind and juice of two lemons

Mix all fruits together; add nutmeg, lemon rind and juice. Add sugar. Melt the Stork and stir into the mixture. Put into clean, warm jars and fasten securely. The mixture makes about three 2 lb jars.

Not everything was rationed but life was often very difficult for Essex households. Rationing was imposed on 8 January 1940 and continued until 1954. During that time an individual was allowed 4oz of bacon; 4oz of butter; 2oz of tea; 2oz of butter and 1oz of cheese per week. Families learned to be economical with their recipes using powered eggs and substituting margarine for butter.

Mince Pies

A favourite tradition of Christmas is the famous mince pie. They were known to exist as early as the late 1500s but in those times, a mixture of mutton and chicken was used together with plenty of spices and raisins. There is a belief that an individual should eat one mince pie on each of the twelve days of Christmas. This will ensure the individual can expect twelve very happy months in the year to come.

Christmas Puddings

The Christmas pudding of today is nothing like the original pudding that began as frumenty, a kind of corn or wheat mixture boiled to perfection. Later, eggs, lumps of meat, prunes and plums were added and the pudding adopted the name of plum pudding. The name stuck even as other ingredients such as sultanas, currants, raisins, eggs and spices were included.

Even with the hustle and bustle of the Christmas holidays today, many people in Essex still prepare their own Christmas puddings in

earthenware basins handed down to them through the generations. They even continue the tradition of asking each family member to stir the mixture three times in a clockwise direction. This is believed to have originated from a biblical association with the Holy Trinity and the Three Wise Men. When all members of the household had completed the task, a silver joey, a threepenny bit, was added to the pudding before it was steamed. Whoever was lucky enough to get the joey in their portion of pudding on Christmas day could expect wealth for the following year.

Essex Sloe Gin

Those people who had small gardens or even allotments grew what they could to supplement their meagre rations. Jack Bartlett from Billericay remembers the sloe gin, made 'country style' that was enjoyed by his family and his neighbours during the holidays:

Ingredients:

1 quart of gin
1½ pints of ripe sloes (should be picked after the first frost)
¾ lbs of sugar
½ oz bitter almonds (blanched and split)

Sloe wine. (Sylvia Kent)

Method:
Place the gin, sugar, bitter almonds and sloes in a pan and stir together. Close with a tight fitting lid and leave for at least three to six months, stirring occasionally. Strain liquid through cheesecloth and bottle. Do not throw away the sloes as they can be chopped and used in mincemeat or fruit cakes.

The Christmas Bird

Although it is generally assumed that a turkey is the standard bird of choice for Christmas dinner, many people during the early 1900s could not afford such a luxury, but those that could often purchased their bird at the local marketplace. Romford Market's location was perfect for Essex farmers who knew they would get a good price for their produce and livestock.

Usually, it was the responsibility of the farm's shepherd to get his turkeys to market in time for Christmas. Mr Baxter, shepherd of Codham Hall Farm, Great Warley, used to make the trek to Romford Market at Christmas, a distance of about six miles. He often took with him his young daughter Eva who recalled the long journey, 'Dad used to herd our turkeys and geese through warm tar which, when it dried and hardened, provided some protection for their little feet on the arduous journey to Romford Market.'

It seems that every kind of bird was accepted as Christmas fare, even the majestic mute swans that were known as 'royal birds' graced the tables of manor houses. The cygnets would be kept and fattened in swan pits ready for the Christmas market. Once they had reached 10-15lbs in weight, the birds would be dressed and sold for as much as two guineas each. The practice of rearing mute swans for the dinner table was still in effect up until the First World War. Now we prefer to watch these beautiful creatures in their natural habitat rather than on our Christmas tables.

It was not only mute swans that became special fodder at Christmas but also skylarks, godwits and pigeons. All have a strong, gamey flavour and require specific preparation and cooking to help keep the birds moist and flavourful. Rich gravy made with sherry or port was also suggested to complement the dish. One of the most popular ways to cook a pigeon was to first sew the bird up at each end to prevent the juices from escaping and then roast it on an open fire. Yet another ancient recipe for stewed pigeons suggests, 'Take peions and stop them with garlic pylled and gode hebres.'

Boar's Head

It would be a mistake to believe that only fowl was used for the Christmas feast. The boar's head was once considered the favourite dish to serve at many houses in Essex; in fact a wrestling match determined who would receive the coveted prize. The boar's head would be served with great ceremony, trumpets sounding the arrival of a large, silver platter containing the boar's head complete with an apple in its mouth as a garnish.

An account in *Handbook to The Environs of London* by James Thorn published in 1876 provides a glimpse into the ancient custom of wrestling for the boar's head and mentioned Hornchurch:

> The church, St. Andrew, on the rt. Of the road at the E. end of the vill., is a large Perp. Building of stone, but patched with brick … on

Boar's head. (Private collection)

the apex of the E. gable is fixed the carved skull of an ox, with broad-spreading curved horns … the horns on the gable of the ch. are commonly supposed to symbolise the name. The received explanation is that the priory founded here by Henry II. As a cell of the Hospice of St. Bernard in Savoy, was called the Monasterium Corutum, and had the head and horns of an ox for a crest … but this of course does not show how the name originated. On the suppression of the alien priories, William of Wykeham purchased the property, with the advowson of the living, for his New College, Oxford, to which it still belongs. A curious custom is maintained here. New College, or the lessee of the

tithes, provides once a year a boar's head, garnished with bay leaves and decorated with ribbons, which is wrestled for in a field adjoining the ch.-yard.

Umble Pie

The lead-up to Christmas was an important event in most households, rich or poor. During the sixteenth century, the more affluent members of society joined with their friends and neighbours to hunt for game for the table. After a successful hunt, the choicest cuts of meat were sent to the cook at the manor house to prepare for the lord and lady of the house and their guests. The less desirable entrails or 'humbles' (sometimes known as 'umbles') were given to the huntsmen and servants as a reward for their services.

Umble pie. (Private collection)

On Christmas Day 1551, it is on record that Lord Petre invited local people and tenants from the estate to join him and some of his staff for dinner. It is recorded that two 'umble pasties' were among the dishes brought to the table. It is known that such pies contained a mixture of heart, liver, kidney and inferior cuts of meat not deemed suitable for the lord and lady's table. Gravy was added to the mixture and it was then topped with a pastry shell. Perhaps the term 'eating humble pie' originated with this early medieval dining custom of feeding the lower orders.

The Essex Pig

Over the centuries our tastes in food have changed drastically. We can now purchase our food pre-wrapped and pre-cooked, but it was not all that long ago that cottagers in Essex provided for their families by living off the land and being completely self-sufficient. Many families owned some livestock, most notably a pig.

The pig was fed and watched carefully at the beginning of the year, but then, in the autumn, it was turned loose into the woods to eat acorns, the grain left after harvesting and any fruit that had fallen to the ground. This custom of turning the pig loose for it to eat 'at will' was called 'pannage' and was recognised throughout England. The custom continued in Epping Forest until the twentieth century.

The Essex pig (The Essex Pig Company)

It was suggested in an old almanac that the time to kill the pig was around Hallontide, 11 November. By harvesting the pig at this time, there was ample time for the meat to be salted and prepared for Christmas holidays. An Essex rhyme:

At Michaelmas safely go stie up the boar
Lest staying abrode, you see him no more;
The sooner the better for Hallontide nie;
And better he brawneth if hard he do lie.

In 1813, Arthur Young describes in his book *General View of the Agriculture of Essex* the 'Essex half black' breed at Felix Hall, Kelvedon. He goes to say, 'the finest breed of hogs that I have seen in Essex, and indeed equal, if not superior to any elsewhere to be found'.

The Essex pig has had a revival of sorts with The Essex Pig Company whose owner has gone to great lengths to bring this rare breed back from almost extinction.

The Orchards at Tiptree

There are few people in Essex who are not aware of the orchards at Tiptree. One of the most popular farms to visit is the Wilkin and Sons Co. at Tiptree. The family has farmed in the area for almost 300 years, but it has only been during the last 120 years that they have

The orchards at Tiptree. (Wilkin & Sons)

been producing the wonderful products so familiar to not only the families of Essex, but a worldwide market. At Christmas time, the puddings, delicious hard sauce and their signature mincemeat recipes have become annual favourites.

Whole generations have worked the farms, the tradition handed down from father to son or daughter and then on to the grandchildren. In the old days, Mr Wilkin rode his horse around the estates inspecting the fruit to be harvested and making sure all was in order. At the lunch hour, a bell at the top of a tower would be rung to indicate that Mr Wilkin's lunch was ready. He would stop for lunch at the farmhouse but would return soon after to continue to his business. Ian Thurgood, joint managing director of Wilkin & Sons Ltd said:

> That dedication to quality is still in effect today. Our Chairman, Peter Wilkin takes a hands-on approach to the daily running of the company. He holds a degree in horticultural and understands the business literally from the ground up. He oversees everything from the orchards to the finished product, therefore continuing the tradition of his grandparents by providing the best quality possible to our customers.
>
> We prepare well ahead for the Christmas market. Our Christmas puddings are a speciality at Tiptree using best quality French brandy and Tawny Marmalade. Topped with our brandy butter, it is a holiday favourite.
>
> Our Christmas Conserve which is a Tiptree signature piece is also a best seller and we must not forget our special blend of vine fruits, apples, citrus peel, spices used in our mincemeat. We begin the process quite early in the year so that the flavours can mix and mature.
>
> Another very old tradition at Christmas time is the medlar. This small fruit is grown in orchards dotted around the Tiptree estate. The

The orchards at Tiptree. (Wilkin & Sons)

fruit has a rough brown-yellow skin, can be as large as a Victoria Plum and has the shape of a rose hip. It is not picked until November and is therefore the last crop for us to harvest at Tiptree. Medlars have been grown in England for centuries and were common in Victorian times when well-to-do-families would have a medlar tree in the garden, pick the fruit and store it in a barn to be eaten as a sweet at Christmas. The fruit is not ripe until the brown pulp can be squeezed from the skin, yet the resulting jelly is a rich red colour and has the flavour of a spiced apple – ideal for use as a jam or as a condiment to meat.

We will continue the legacy of providing the best quality products to our customers, not just at Christmas but year round.

Candied Eryngo – An Essex Delight!

The Eryngo plant, sometimes known as sea holly, has a long and fascinating history. It was known to have been used as a medicine as early as the first century AD by Dioscorides, a Greek scholar. He believed the plant helped with gastrointestinal ailments and other related problems. In medieval times the root became very popular among English aristocracy because some believed it had aphrodisiac powers. The delicacy was also mentioned in works by William Shakespeare and the diarist, John Evelyn.

In Colchester, the process of candying the root became a lucrative market for Robert Buxton, a local apothecary. He kept the process of candying the root a closely guarded secret that remained in the Buxton family for years. On Buxton's death in 1655, the recipe was handed down to an employee, Samuel Great who continued producing the delicacy all the while maintaining the secrecy he promised Buxton.

Eryngo was so important to the town of Colchester; it was presented to Princess Charlotte of Mecklenburg-Strelitz when she visited the town in August, 1761. Princess Charlotte was on route from Harwich to marry King George III, but had stopped in Colchester for refreshments. The *London Gazette* reported:

> About five o'clock she came to Colchester and stopped at the house of Mr Enew, where she was received and waited upon by Mrs Enew and Mrs Ribow … Mr Great of Colchester had the honour of pre-

senting to her Majesty, while she was at Mr Enew's house, a box of candied eringo-root.

It is said the eryngo roots, once washed, boiled or roasted, have a flavour similar to chestnuts, whilst candied, they resemble a liquorice twist. The delicacy was also known as sweetmeats and was affectionately called 'kissing comfits'.

Stir up Sunday and Twelfth Night Cake

The last Sunday before Advent is known as 'Stir up Sunday' so called from the first two words, 'Stir up, O Lord; we beseech Thee, the hearts of Thy Faithful people.' This opening prayer (or Collect) was meant to stir the emotions of the faithful, to prepare them for the coming of Christ and welcoming Him into their hearts.

During the 1850s, the Victorians fully embraced the Christmas spirit not only with special prayers, but they also started the tradition of bringing a fir tree into the home and decorating it with lighted candles. It was Queen Victoria's husband, Prince Albert, who saw the custom in his native Germany and liked it so much; he brought the idea to England where it flourished. At first, it was just the nobility who erected a tree in their homes, but later, the working classes also began celebrating Christmas by bringing branches of evergreens into their homes and using them as decoration.

Stir Up Sunday and Twelfth Night cake. (Donald Wallace)

The holidays have always involved those special foods such as mince pies, rum sauce and Christmas cake. The cake was prepared weeks in advance traditionally on the last Sunday before Advent and cut on twelfth night, 6 January. Hidden in the cake was a bean or sometimes a small trinket. The man or woman who found the token would be proclaimed the lord or lady of the evening. The celebrations would entail mock ceremonies and provide harmless entertainment for everyone at the party.

The seventeenth-century poet Robert Herrick wrote of the Twelfth Night Cake and the king bean tradition:

Now, now, the mirth comes
With the cake full of plums,
Where bean is the king of the sport here;
Beside we must know,
The pea also
Must revel as queen in the court here.

Begin then to choose
This night as ye use,
Who shall for the present delight here;
Be a king by the lot,
And who shall not
Be Twelfth-day Queen for the night here.

By Robert Herrick

Eva Baxter, now sadly departed, stated that as a child, she remembered Stir up Sundays and she as she and her friends sang on their way home from a church service at Great Warley:

Stir up, we beseech thee,
The pudding in the pot,
And when we get home
We'll eat it all hot.

Holiday Cheer

During the fifteenth and sixteenth centuries, Romford and the surrounding areas were known for the tanneries, in fact there was a common expression, 'Go to Romford to be new-bottomed'. This meant that Romford was the place to go for new leather breeches but over time, the main industry would change from leatherworks to brewers.

When Edward Ind purchased 'The Star' brewery in 1799, he could not have imagined the success, wealth and notoriety it would bring him. He changed the name and so began the legacy of the Ind Coope Brewery in Romford. By the early 1900s, approximately 450 people were employed at the Romford location followed quickly by a second successful brewery in Burton-on-Trent.

The success of the brewery in Romford was due in part to the railway line that ran close to the plant therefore allowing workers fast and easy access. This allowed workers to commute to the brewery from outlying towns by purchasing workman's cheap day return ticket. Ind Coope employed their own workmen including wheelwrights, carpenters and stablemen in fact, they were completely self-sufficient.

Wassailing

The ancient custom of wassailing is still practiced in Essex, notably in Saffron Walden. The name comes from the Old English term 'waes hael' meaning 'be well.' Wassail is an ale-based drink sweetened with honey and seasoned with spices. Traditionally, the bowl of ale was passed around with the greeting 'Wassail'. Sometimes a carol was sung:

Wassailing. (Wilkin & Sons)

Here we come a-wassailing
Among the leaves so green,
Here we come a-wassailing,
So fair to be seen:

Love and joy come to you,
And to you your wassail too,
And God bless you and send you,
A happy New Year,
And God send you,
A happy New Year.

Award Winning Mead

Sylvia Kent, an Essex author, is also a well-known wine maker in Billericay. In 1993, her mead recipe won the Essex Amateur Wine-making Federation's Mead Cup. Her recipe is simple:

Mead

3lbs of honey
1 teaspoon All Purpose Yeast
1 teaspoon grape tannin
1 teaspoon tartaric acid
8 pints (1 gallon) boiled water, cooled.

Method:

Sterilise all equipment with 1 campden tablet dissolved in half pint boiled water.
Activate 1 teaspoon all purpose yeast by mixing with 1 teaspoon sugar, half pint warm water, mix well and put in a sterilised bottle, leave for 2 hours to start work.
Meanwhile pour honey into demi-john with 1 teaspoon tartaric acid, 1 teaspoon grape tannin and 7 pints water.
Add the fermenting yeast to the demi-john, shake well, add an airlock and allow to ferment in a warm atmosphere, adding the last pint of

Award-winning mead.
(Victoria Wallace)

cooled, boiled water when initial froth has subsided. Allow the gallon of liquid to ferment in a warm place until fermentation is complete – could take 6 weeks or so, then rack off into another sterilised demi-john. Add a campden tablet and store in a cold place to mature for six months at least.

Harold Wood Hospital

★

Harold Wood Hospital, Ward No. 2, Christmas 1953. (Mrs Betty Pether)

Harold Wood Hospital located on Gubbins Lane in Harold Wood is now closed, but memories linger on. This photograph taken on Christmas Day 1953 shows the extraordinary efforts the staff took to make the day as

cheery as possible for their patients. Decorations hang from every light fixture in the form of butterflies, glitter and balloons. The large Christmas tree in the center is surrounded by tables holding special gifts and treats. Each patient has a small fairy doll sitting on the tray on their beds, and a large owl sits in the foreground as if watching over the celebrations – such pleasant memories!